8

ALSO BY AMY FUSSELMAN

The Pharmacist's Mate

8

amy fusselman

COUNTERPOINT

A MEMBER OF THE PERSEUS BOOKS GROUP

NEW YORK

Books published by Counterpoint books are available at special discounts
for bulk purchases in the United States by corporations, institutions, and
other organizations. For more information, please contact the Special
Markets Department at the Perseus Books Group, 11 Cambridge Center,
Cambridge MA 02142, or call (617) 252-5298 or (800) 255-1514, or
e-mail special.markets@perseusbooks.com.

Designed by Jeff Williams
Set in 11.5-point Bembo

Library of Congress Cataloging-in-Publication Data
    Fusselman, Amy.
    8 : all true unbelievable / Amy Fusselman.
      p. cm.
    ISBN-13: 978-1-58243-368-4
    ISBN-10: 1-58243-368-2
I. Title. II. Title: Eight : all true unbelievable.

PS3606.U86Z46 2007
814'.6—dc22
                                                            2006037747

10 9 8 7 6 5 4 3 2 1

For King

Events in time are not—boom—over. They have tentacles, and they wrap around, and they swish back and forth, and they sink and swim.

Things in time exist like this because of the nature of time itself, which is plastic, and around and in the human body at all times, like air.

I believe this—I believe that we are alive in the most fantastic pliable medium, time, and yet I sometimes find myself unable to convince myself that it is possible for anything new and different to happen in a human life. It's all same old, same old.

The problem, I think, is that I understand what events in time do when they are here—I understand their swimming and lingering. What I don't understand is how events in time get here. I don't understand how things happen.

I used to think it was simple—people perform actions. Things happen because an invisible force inside people—

human will—makes its way outside people, thereby becoming visible.

As I have gotten older I have seen that this single, rocket-ship-like, inside-to-outside model is only one of many explanations for how things can happen.

Other explanations I try to keep in mind now:

—there are other forces in the world besides human will

—there is a divine force in the world that can't be located in one place, that is simultaneously inside and outside and up and down and around and back and forth.

Whether a force is divine or human, though, the rule is the same: you can't see the energy. You see what it moves, and how.

8

There are exceptions to the rule, however. There are peo-ple who can see the energy. They can see, for instance, what looks like a small river rushing around the edge of each finger, when they spread their hands out in front of them.

You wouldn't believe the things people can do, really.

8

Understanding how things happen is not easy. The rocket-ship image of a page ago is a super-simplification: it doesn't take into account the fact that human beings not only have the ability to do two things at one time, but that they have the ability to do two things at one time that are at cross-purposes.

People can read books and watch children at the same time, for instance. Of course, both the reading of the books and the watching of the children will be performed in a way best described as half-assed. If you want to read your book in a non-half-assed way, you have to wait until your child is in kindergarten, or you must pay someone to watch your child while you read your book. Even then, however, you must not read the book in your home because your child will find you and jump on you and make reading impossible. You must leave your home, leave your yard, leave your street. You must drive to a café in town to read your book.

You must run and hide from your child as if your child is serving you a subpoena.

This is not insane. It does not make you bad if you do this.

If you have a child, you already know this. You already know that you can't watch your child and simultaneously read books because you must give your child everything. But not everything-everything like you may have come to think of it: not every toy, every convenience, every whim; not every shred of yourself until you are resentful and exhausted. To be really healthy, to be really balanced, you are supposed to keep a little bit of yourself for yourself. Perhaps you are able to do this.

Let's just assume, however, that you are not. You have not been able to keep from giving your kids every shred of your energy, your will, your time. Then most likely you are already aware of something else that has happened to you: you have become a robot. The number of times you are repeating the same few actions: doing laundry, picking up toys, wiping bottom, picking up baby, saying stop, saying eat, saying come here now, put on your shoes, etc.: it is incalculable. It is hundreds of thousands of times per child.

You must be a robot because you care for a child. Children are wild! If they are under age five in particular—wild!

Out of their minds! They are only cute because they are small. If they were big they would be terrifying. They would be in jail. They are in jail now, really: cribs, exersaucers, strollers, highchairs. They are escorted, like prisoners, everywhere. And in their jail, which is your jail, you robot-sing them songs with robot motions: ABC twinkly spider bus. What play are you in, who wrote these words, these gestures? Is this a tragedy?

It could be a tragedy. The thing that keeps it from being a tragedy, that turns it into a comedy, or at least a musical, is your robot-self. You have to be very careful with your robot-self. The way in which you perform your hundred thousand repetitive actions is incredibly important. You must become the most fabulous robot you can be. This is not easy. You can't do it with your brain. You can't read your way into it, I am sorry to say.

What do you do, then?

First, you must be aware of something: the way that humans learn. Humans learn through repetition. We are tied to time this way. We are shackled to it; we move through it. Even before we have a complete skeleton, we exist in time. Time is our name: nine weeks, twelve weeks.

Time is a greater mother to us than our own mothers.

Time is inside and outside us, it is the fantastic sea we move through, capable of the most astonishing bends and whorls and, of course, like most things that are magical and wild and inside us, we have reduced it to something small and controllable outside us. Time is not magical, we say. Time is the annoying thing I wear on my wrist. Time is the thing that ticks on without me. Time is the round sculpture on the wall with numbers that I look at occasionally to help me figure out where I am in my day. Time is like a map. I have to take it out of my pocket and look at it with my eyes and then I use my brain and I think about it and I do a little computation and that is that; I know where I am now. Thank you, Time.

This is the wrong model.

Time is inside humans and outside humans and they learn in it. Their learning cannot be divorced from it. Which is to say they learn—tick tick tick—by doing the same thing over and over until they are good at it or they abandon it.

This robot side of parenting, unfortunately, is usually discounted. No, you are not a robot, the books imply, of course you are not a robot, you are a human, a loving and caring and kind and wonderful and not unfeeling human.

The robot part is then explained as if the parents don't know it already. The books say to robot this and robot that, put the baby on robot schedule, robot food, robot sleep, sing robot, poop robot. Attach robot.

I say embrace your robot. Embrace the repetition of this work. You are a machine your children love and fear. You are a robot god.

It is scary. Was your mother a robot?
Yes.

But we are not robots, you say. We could be, it would be fine if we were, we are not afraid of robots. See? We love them! They are our pets!

They're not us, though.

Look, this is not a problem to be fixed. Robots have fantastic attributes:

   —predictability
   —efficiency
   —responsiveness
   —cleanliness
   —strength
   —the ability to bear loss without breaking

8

Pedophiles are so crazy. I know this because I had one. I had a pedophile of my very own. He was the husband of a woman who babysat me. The babysitter's name was Mrs. Dauth, she was a Jesus freak. The pedophile's name was Mr. Dauth. I don't know what his first name was. He's most likely dead now. He was sixty-some when this happened, and that was almost forty years ago. I was four, the same age my oldest son is now. I have two boys. The older one is named King. The younger one is named Lyons, but we call him Mick or Mickey.

Mr. _____ Dauth was driving me to ballet class in Connecticut, where we lived. My parents were on vacation in Florida, and Mr. and Mrs. Dauth were staying in our house. I was in the front of the car, in the passenger seat. I wasn't wearing a seat belt because nobody cared about that then. I was sitting with my left leg flat on the seat, in a triangle, and my right leg on the floor, so that I was facing him.

I was screaming at him that he was going to go to hell. We were in traffic and the windows were open. It was spring.

He laughed at me. He told me I was crazy to believe in hell, that hell did not exist.

I remember continuing to scream at him, "Yes it does! Yes it does exist!"

He continued to tell me—he wasn't screaming, he was talking and laughing—"No, it doesn't, it is made-up. It is a story."

As we continued in this vein I remember feeling a growing sense of excitement. We were having a conversation. We were talking about a serious matter, whether hell existed or not. This was something adults talked about. This was one of the most serious conversations of my entire childhood. This was as seriously as anyone in my childhood had ever taken me.

8

We learn through repetition. But we never learn that what we do, over and over, is a thing. If what we are doing is changing the diaper, wiping the baby, over and over, touching the baby with the intention to clean, this action is itself a body, it exists in time, and it exists separately from the product that we see as a result of these actions: a clean baby. The touching with the intention to clean, this is a real thing in time, in space. It is a thing. It rings out in circles; it is like a tree. It is as real as a tree in a forest of trees. A hundred thousand times, we touched the baby, we wiped the baby, we cleaned the baby. When the baby is no longer a baby, when the baby is a child and no longer wears diapers, when the child is toilet trained and all the wiping, the diapers are a memory, when the diapers are gone—well, not gone, but difficult to locate, let's say, groaning anonymously under the great rotating drum of the landfill compactor on the mountain of trash—at that moment when everything about the touching appears to have been lost, it is not lost. It's just that we can't see it.

But it exists. It's like a lake of bright blue air that grownup and child are in together, a lake of 100,000 touches that we walk in, up the stairs to the prekindergarten class, where we kiss a butterfly kiss and say goodbye. And then, without knowing it in words, we do something miraculous, which is part the water. And each of us takes our bit of the lake away until next time.

8

Why do adults have no imagination? Why do they have so many problems thinking that things could be different? What do they have invested in keeping things the same?

Just their whole world, I guess. I am an adult. I should use a different possessive. Just my whole world.

I keep going back and forth on that, though: on whose world it is, and how old I am.

8

When I was a child, I danced a lot. I felt very full with music. I let the music come into my body, I let it become something body-shaped.

When you dance, people walk around you wider, give you more room, a wider berth. You are dancing; it's hard to predict what you are going to do next. You might jump. You might twirl.

My mom saw that I was dancing a lot, and at the time my dad was taking figure skating lessons, so she got me involved in figure skating. Eventually, after I finished kindergarten, we moved to Minneapolis, where my pedophile did not follow. They had a lot of winter sports up there in Minnesota, a lot of skating rinks. My mom liked to keep me busy. I skated a lot. By the time I was ten, I usually skated four or five hours a day.

There is one part of skating that is not emphasized as much as it should be: the speed. They try to ballet-ify skating, and make skaters like ballerinas, only more Broadway-ish. But really what they should do is have one of those speedometers out there like what you see on the highway, when you pass the big digital readout and it says 90 when you should be going 55. They should have that as skaters go by in their ballerina outfits so we have a big lit-up number to remind us how fast they are going. Or maybe they could ditch the ballerina-style in favor of jet outfits. Figure skaters should always wear big silver bodysuits a la speed skaters. Aerodynamic. Or better yet, figure skaters should shave their whole bodies, like swimmers, and then skate naked. And then we could have the big digital lit-up number to show how fast the muscular, naked, shaved skater-ballerinas are going.

I never did anything like that, though. Instead, I went to skating competitions and skated as ballerina-y as possible to songs like "If I Were a Rich Man" while wearing glittering, faux-peasant outfits.

8

I recently saw Todd Robbins, the amazing and charismatic sideshow entertainer/sword-swallower/lightbulb-eater/ magician perform at Monday Night Magic, a weekly magic show that takes place in a church ten blocks from me, on 46th Street.

"I am the most honest charlatan you will ever meet," he told us, before revealing the trick behind swallowing a sword: practice. One bends a coat hanger into a sword shape, and then ingests it seven times each morning and seven times each night, until at last one conquers the gag reflex.

After explaining the regimen behind it, Todd swallowed an exceedingly long sword, and then, in a gesture he did not explain, took a bow with it inside him, the handle curlicuing out of his mouth like a silver tongue.

8

Let's make this fast. I had a pedophile and then I didn't and then I skated for a long time and then I quit skating and then I started drinking and then I quit drinking and then I started therapy and then I got married and then I still had therapy and then I had children and then I still had therapy and finally I decided I was tired of all this therapy, all this talking like a talk machine; I wanted someone to lay their hands on me.

8

I talked to my mom on the phone yesterday and she told me she had thrown away some clay. When I was a child in Connecticut, my mom was a potter. She had her own wheel, she made beautiful things. Then when we moved to

Minneapolis from Connecticut, she sold her wheel, ostensibly because there was no space, and then for years after that she bemoaned selling it. She never got a new one, though.

I didn't know she had saved any clay. But yes, she said, it was clay from Connecticut, forty years old, like me. She had saved it in a copper boiler that had been given to her by my father's parents. She had moved it from Connecticut to Minneapolis and then from Minneapolis to Ohio, where we had moved when I finished sixth grade, and where my parents stayed together until my father died a few years ago.

She was calling, she said, to ask if I wanted the copper boiler.

I said yes.

Then she told me: she had taken the saved clay out of the copper boiler and put it on a little cart she had in the garage, and pushed it out the garage door, down the path outside her condo, until she got to the back of the neighbor's condo, which is slightly higher up the hill than hers.

Behind my mother's and the neighbor's condos, there is a drop off of about twenty feet, into a little creek. My mother went to the highest point behind the neighbor's condo, with the cart, and took the saved clay off the cart, and set it down on the grass. Then she stood there, and kicked the forty-year-old clay off the edge of the hill so that it rolled down into the creek.

She stood there. She said she imagined the clay in the water, slowly dissolving, and then flowing down to the pond and, "Oh, I don't know," she said a little uneasily, "maybe making the fish happy."

8

I had been in therapy talking for years. I had had young, old, middle-aged, Gestalt, and Freudian therapists. I had had a woman who was getting her Masters in Social Work. I had had one guy, very early on, when I was a junior in college—I think he was a student volunteer. I was twenty, he couldn't have been more than twenty-three.

I had talked to a lot of nice women and one young man. But finally, it was like, enough already, it's not sinking in.

I looked up "hands-on healing" on the internet and, lo and behold, there is a lot written about hands-on healing, and in fact one of the foremost American practitioners of this type of healing has written a couple of books. Her name is Barbara Brennan, and she even has a school in Florida.

So I bought one of her books and read it. It was something about energy, how hands-on healers move the energy in your body around and make you more balanced, clear the bad stuff out. I read it in the half-assed way you read things when you are reading and watching small children. All I know is that the book really made me want to try to find someone who could do this, so I went back to the internet, to the Barbara Brennan web site, and I looked on the Barbara Brennan School alumni page and found an alumnus with a name I liked in the city where I live now, New York City, and the alum was a woman and she was a healer and a singer and I thought that felt right, so I emailed her about having a healing and she wrote me back and said she didn't live in New York City anymore but she knew someone who did and I should go and see him, and that pretty much ground me to a halt right there.

I couldn't imagine going to a man for a hands-on healing. Now that I am a grown-up, I always prefer women when it comes to anything healing-related. I have a female OB, female dentist, female pediatrician, female primary care physician, everything.

But I looked over the alumni list again, and no other names seemed right, so I waited a month or two, and finally the desire for this hands-on thing did not go away and

I screwed my courage up and called this guy, his name was Vincent De Rosa, and I explained that I got his number through this lady that no longer lived here and I told him my story, or some of it, and then I said I was interested in having a healing but worried because he was a man. So we arranged to meet at a coffee shop just to talk about the possibility of my doing this. Healing, that is. I wasn't promising I would do this, I said. Especially when I heard he worked out of his apartment.

I felt like I was having an affair, going to this meeting. I didn't tell anyone about it. Not my husband Frank, not Chandra our babysitter, not any of my friends. I knew what Frank would say about my going to a hands-on healer: he would say I was out of my mind. He would ask me why I thought we had money to spend on crap like that. And if he knew the healer was a man he would extra, extra not like it. So I didn't tell him, which felt weird. And then I didn't tell any of my friends because I knew they would think I was crazy. Who wants to admit they want this kind of healing? Most people who want this, I think, get massages or have sex. What Marvin Gaye sings about.

But that wasn't it, it wasn't about sex. Sex is another animal. And it wasn't just about being touched like in massage; it wasn't about making my muscles feel better, or "relaxing." It was about being touched with a very specific intention: an intention to heal. This is not the same thing as going to a doctor. Doctors, in my experience, touch you with the desire to examine you, and then they use their brains to figure out what to do. This is fine, but right then it wasn't what I wanted. What I wanted was to lie there and not use my brain, and believe someone was trying to help me, also not with his or her brain.

I understand how this sounds. But you have to remember that I had been trying to use my brain on my problems for twenty years. For the last three years I had sat on the couch and used my brain and spoken with a female Doctor of Psychology—a female MSW candidate was not enough anymore, thank you—who was also using her brain. I was over my brain. I was over everybody's brain. I wanted some other organ involved. Heart would be nice. But I would take spleen, to be honest.

I made sure I got to the coffee shop early so I could watch Vincent De Rosa walk in. I thought no one knows where I am—what if he is an axe murderer? Already he knows my phone number. Already he knows I am vulnerable and scared and crazy, because only vulnerable, scared, crazy people want to go to healers who don't use their brains. What if he is really nice and then I go have a healing from him but instead he chains me to the radiator?

Vincent had told me he would be wearing a tan coat, and he was. It was a tan Carhartt coat, he looked lumberjacky. I watched him kiss an Asian woman goodbye.

I thought that was a good sign, watching him kiss her. Usually axe murderers are single, I thought.

So he came in and sat down across the table from me and he had this smile that was very soft and bright, it reminded me of a musician I know who was a rock star and then he quit drinking and started singing children's songs and now he is a much better children's song-singer than he ever was as a rock star.

We talked awhile and I told him I had this urge to have this kind of hands-on healing, that I had been in therapy for awhile and was just sick of talking. And I told him about the pedophile, and that I was scared to work with him because he was a guy.

He listened to me, and made some suggestions, and then we worked out this plan where I would come to his apartment for a healing, but his girlfriend—the Asian woman—would be there, and she would stay there the whole time.

I don't know why this made me feel safe, the girlfriend could just as easily have been another axe murderer, and why, considering my experience, do I think women are going to save me from being raped?

I don't know. But at the appointed time on the appointed day without telling anyone I walked in the door of one apartment among the hundreds of apartments in one building among the cluster of buildings known as Stuyvesant Town, and then I immediately went to their bathroom and peed because I had had a lot of coffee already, and their bathroom looked like someone had gone to the trouble of carefully cleaning it and closing the shower curtain so you could not see the bathtub—something people often do when you go to open houses in their apartments, because people's tubs are not always gleamy clean. It was like the bathroom had a sense of decorum. I liked that.

So I met the girlfriend, whose name was Sanghi, and she had a similar feel as Vincent—open and smiling, warm—and she asked me if it was OK if she sat and typed on the computer during my healing, and I said absolutely, it's great, I actually find that tappity-tap sound very comforting, and she and Vincent both laughed at that.

Then I sat with Vincent and told him a little bit about what was going on with me, sort of like he was a friend, and then I took off my shoes and climbed on his table, a massage table, and tried to decide whether I wanted the pillow under my head or not (not) as Sanghi clicked on the keyboard and I worked up the courage to close my eyes.

Vincent had explained that he would hold my feet for a second, and then the rest of the time he would not touch my body, but his hands would be near my body. He would only touch my feet. That was actually what sealed the deal for me, as far as hands-on healing went: he would touch me, but not too much.

I was wearing socks, he touched my feet, the keys clicked.

After a minute he let go of my feet and moved his hands somewhere else, I don't know where.

8

I am writing this section later, after I thought I had finished writing this whole book. I realized I left some things hanging and I needed to go back and tie them up. It's a pain to have to go back when you think you are done, but I have an image to inspire me: Grave Digger, the monster truck.

Monster trucks have come into my life in a big way in the last year. Someone gave us a toy one first, for

King, who loved it. And then gradually we bought more toy ones for both boys and then we got a book or two and then we bought more toy ones and then we got a video and then we looked at footage on the internet and gradually I have learned about monster trucks, about their names and actions and which trucks are famous for what.

And I was following along in this seminar on monster trucks, just as I have followed along in every other crash course the boys have led me through—the course on trains happened a couple of years ago; the one on sea creatures was more recent—and I was bobbing along in the river of obsessive interest around monster trucks, not exactly loving it any more or less than any other river-of-interest we had floated along, and then one evening, as part of it, Frank and I sat with both boys on the couch and watched internet videos we downloaded of monster trucks performing at monster truck shows.

If you don't know already, monster trucks are gigantic trucks—usually pickups but sometimes other kinds—that have been modified with extremely large tires and suspension systems. Monster trucks are also a lot like figure skaters in that they basically exist for the purpose of performing in front of an audience.

Monster truck shows happen all over the United States, although I have yet to see one in Manhattan. The primary components of the shows are racing and freestyle. In the racing event, trucks are pitted against each other; in freestyle, each truck performs alone. The shows typically happen in the same type of coliseum or arena where one would watch figure skaters except that rather than pristine white ice covering the floor there is mud, dirt, ramps, and piles of old cars that have been carefully arranged in preparation for being jumped on and demolished.

We sat there, watching these internet videos of trucks doing their freestyle programs, and pretty soon it became clear that the monster truck repertoire is somewhat limited, like figure skating, to certain prescribed movements. Akin to a figure skater's spin, for example, there is the monster truck's donut, which is usually performed in a dusty part of the arena to create as much of a dirt cyclone as possible. Other monster truck movements include wheelies and jumps, the latter of which are traditionally performed by speeding off a dirt ramp and landing on the aforementioned piles of old cars.

The trucks that we saw on the internet performed their tricks competently, gunning their engines and making a ton of noise, jumping and bouncing and spinning. It's all tremendously loud and dirty, and you hear the giant engines roar and you hear the crowd yelling and clapping and you know intellectually that it's dangerous for the drivers, who are encased inside the trucks in roll cages and eighteen-point-harnesses and flameproof suits and helmets, but after awhile it seems slightly slow and—though this seems impossible, intellectually—boring. At times, I could not help thinking it was exactly like watching a giant metal puppy repeatedly jumping onto a pile of giant metal pillows.

Perhaps this is partly because the human element is muted in these performances. You can't see the drivers very well, so the trucks, which are often adorned with facial features along their front ends—do tend to seem like their own mechanical beings. And despite their flaming paint jobs and ferocious names—e.g., Bigfoot or Carolina Crusher—most of the trucks really just seemed like very nice figure skaters who were primarily interested in landing their jumps competently and not falling down.

And then we watched Grave Digger, and Grave Digger made us—me and Frank, that is—cry. (King and Mick did not cry, they got excited, and wanted to watch Grave Digger again and again).

What made Grave Digger different?

Basically, Grave Digger was operating under an entirely different value system. Rather than trying primarily not to fall down, Grave Digger pretty much entered the arena falling down. The video we saw on the internet was entitled "Grave Digger Goes Ballistic" and was completely different from any other monster truck video we saw in that Grave Digger did not seem to be concerned with any rules the other trucks had played by at all. In fact, we weren't even really aware that the other trucks were playing by any rules until we saw Grave Digger break them. He drove willy-nilly over the ramps rather than jumping off them as intended. He careened insanely and crookedly off the cars that the other trucks had politely and symmetrically bounced on. He seemed to seek the crash that the other trucks were avoiding. He came precariously close to rolling over several times before finally rolling over for good, like a beetle struggling on its shiny black back, at which point the men of the emergency crew came running full speed onto the arena floor, fire extinguishers in hand.

The soundtrack for Grave Digger's performance was also different from the other monster trucks, in that the crowd response to Grave Digger was much, much louder. People were screaming. People were freaking out. Grave Digger was freaking out. He was not being cautious, not paying attention to the laws, not caring about what he was supposed to do, or how, he was FREAKING OUT. He was giving his fans what they wanted, he was giving until there was nothing left, until he ruined what we all agreed was his precious, polished, perfect truck—until he tore it up so badly it wouldn't move anymore.

We weren't even there, in person; we were watching a crappy internet video, and we felt it: the force of a big, metal puppy-truck's crazy, reckless, no-holds-barred giving. It was the kind of thing that makes you think, if you're old like me: this is something to remember. This is something to live by.

8

My PhD-receiving therapist was asking me about memories of my mom and I was saying the thing I remember most about her is being with her in the car. We drove places together. We drove to skating, we drove to ballet, we drove to school, we drove to skating competitions, we

drove to Grandma's, we drove and drove. I sat in the back-
seat and she sat in the front. We sat like this ostensibly
because I needed more space—in the mornings when we
drove it was 5:30 a.m. and I needed to lie down and rest;
after school when we drove I needed to change from my
school clothes to my skating clothes and so I had to crouch
down in the back. My mother and I had our separate jobs
in the car. We were not equals, like when I drove with my
pedophile. We did not have conversations about whether
hell existed or not. In fact, we did not speak that much. In
fact, I don't believe we even listened to music. If there was
anything on it was the radio, but it was turned to the sta-
tion that plays the bingy-bing sound and then says "Give
us twenty minutes and we'll give you the world."

We were usually in the car for longer than twenty minutes.
For all the thousands of hours I spent at skating rinks we
never lived closer than a thirty-minute drive to any rink.
That meant at least an hour in the car every day, more
often two hours.

She drove OK. I never remember her being in a fender
bender. She seemed like a competent driver. She seemed—
happy?—no, not quite happy—calm. Calm while driving.
Maybe that was happiness for her. Maybe she felt like she
was a competent mom when she drove. In charge, in the
driver's seat.

I myself have not driven all that much in my life. I got my license when I was sixteen, but at that time I had already moved out of our house in Ohio and was at a boarding school nearby, so I didn't really drive except when I came home once a month, and I sometimes tried not to come home but to go visit another girl's house instead. I did drive for the summer I spent at home before I went to college, and of course I got into a fender-bender during that time, in a parking lot of a bar when I was supposed to be doing something really edifying—going to see a Brecht play, as I remember—and my fear of getting caught at the bar made me drive away from the accident, which made the other party take my license number, which meant that everything was fine that evening but then a month later the police knocked on the door and told my dad that I had dinged someone's car in a parking lot and driven off, which made my dad about as mad at me as I had ever seen him, and that included the year I was seven, when I woke up at 4 a.m. and opened my Christmas presents while the rest of my family was still asleep.

I was in boarding school where I didn't drive and then I went to college in Ohio and I didn't have a car, and then I lived in Boston and New York City where you don't need cars, so it's really only been in the last few years, when Frank and I had kids and started taking little trips out of the city, that I have driven consistently.

At dinner today I told King that he could not have choco-late milk unless he did nice sitting at the table consistently and then I asked him if he knew what "consistently" meant and he asked me what does it mean, and I said "over time." I thought he was going to ask me what "over time" meant, it's a strange phrase, but he didn't. And then later when I asked him again, "What does consistently mean?" He said it without my reminding him: "over time."

I like the idea of over time. It's as if you are hopping over it, like a rabbit, somehow escaping its structure. You fly over it. But that's exactly what it doesn't mean. It means you are in it, so in it that you act in it, you repeat in it. Maybe that's where the over comes from, because that is really the theory, that it's in the repetition that you find freedom, that anything meaningful only happens as a result of repetition: your heart beating, for instance, or your working on something, or saying hello. It's a result of doing the same things over and over that there is any story at all to our lives, that anything happens. If we were never con-sistent, the theory goes, life would just be a giant wrecked salad bar, an insane smorgasbord, chaos.

I wonder if it is really within our power, though, to never be consistent.

I wonder what, exactly, is really within our power.

8

Another weird thing about figure skating that doesn't get a lot of play anymore is that there is an actual figure part of it. In order to advance in figure skating, to compete on more and more difficult levels, you have to do figures. This is not metaphorical. When you talk about "doing figures" in figure skating, you are talking about writing the number 8 with your feet. You have to write giant number 8s— the size of which are calculated roughly by your height— and you have to try and trace over your writing exactly, so all the lines look like one line, or as close to one line as possible. As you progress up the difficulty ladder you add flourishes to your 8s—loops or brackets, for instance. These terms, again, are not metaphorical. A bracket looks like this: }

Every figure skater who is good enough to be televised in a sparkling outfit doing gigantic spinning jumps at 35 miles per hour has done literally hundreds and hundreds of hours of this—writing with his/her feet. It is not televised, although it is a skater's ability to perform these 8s that determines whether or not said skater can even compete in a televised competition.

This was the way it was, anyway, when I was figure skating in the 1970s. But I just called the United States

Figure Skating Association's offices in Colorado Springs to double-check that this is, in fact, the way things still are, and the very nice lady on the phone told me, "Um, no." The USFSA, she said, basically abolished figures in 1992.

I gasped, then asked her why.

She chose her words carefully: "It wasn't a revenue stream for them," she said.

"So do kids today do figures at all?" I asked, feeling, like, ninety years old.

"Very rarely," she said.

I called Frank. "I can't believe that this thing I spent hundreds and hundreds of hours doing no longer exists," I said. "It's like a gramophone or something."

He was working. He is a video editor, which means he looks at very small increments of video very closely. He can see little details in films, on TV, that I can't see at all.

"Things change," he said.

8

As I am writing this right now, at the Starbucks on 9th Avenue and 47th Street, Oksana Baiul, the Olympic figure skater/drunk-driver/platinum-blond hellion, is sitting across the seating area from me, ordering her doppio without getting back in line, just raising her voice to request it from the barrista, who's lounging against the machine. I want to say something to her about skating and drinking and monster trucks, but I don't know what. I don't think I will say anything, though. I have learned this through bitter experience, living in New York: you should not approach celebrities unless you have a really good excuse. Because if you just go up to them and spew your love at them, even though you may feel good in the moment because your heart can be really full, in the end you will feel terrible when they look at you like you are an idiot.

Hi, Oksana, I won't bother you.

8

When King was two, a few months before Mick was born, we went through this period with him where we did what the sleep-training experts call sleep training. It wasn't really sleep training so much as don't-move training, though. We had to do it because we needed the crib for Mick, so we had to move King out of the crib and into a twin bed. And of course, King quickly discovered

that he could get out of the twin bed. So we started having to do this thing where we sat in his bedroom with
him at night until he fell asleep. Basically if we didn't sit
right next to his bed until he was asleep, he would try to
get out of bed. We were scared he was never going to
learn how to fall asleep alone, so we decided to do this
thing we read about—the sleep training—where you put
the kid to bed and then walk out of the bedroom. And
then each time the kid comes out, you don't look at him,
don't smile at him, don't talk, just take his hand and lead
him back into bed. The idea is that once the kid knows
that he isn't going to get any social interaction, he will
give up and just go to sleep. According to the book, it was
only supposed to take a few nights of doing this before
the kid got the message.

So the first night Frank did it. King went to bed at 8:15,
and between 8:15 and 9:15 he got out of bed—Frank
counted—seventy-six times. On the seventy-sixth time, he
finally stayed in bed and went to sleep.

We agreed to take turns, so the second night, I did it. At
the time I remember being scared that I wasn't going to be
able to do the part of the sleep training that required me
to be an automaton. I was afraid I was not going to be able
to not look at King, and I would instead smile at him. I was
still a new mom then.

My night came and I did it. The whole thing took about an hour, from 8:00 to 9:00. It was hard at first. King came bounding out of his bedroom and stood there in the hallway at the edge of the kitchen with a giant smile on his face. I looked at the wall behind him, and used my peripheral vision to find his hand and then took him by the hand back into bed.

In the beginning I decided I was going to try to do the sleep training and also try to read something in the paper in the moments when I came back to the kitchen and could stand at the table for a few seconds, but it became clear pretty quickly that that was not going to be possible. I had to surrender to the sleep training and not do anything else. The whole process was very active. No sooner had I gotten King back into bed, under the covers, and smoothed the covers over his back and patted his back twice—the only real expression I allowed myself to give him—and walked back to the kitchen table, his little footsteps were going pat-pat and he was at the edge of the kitchen again. It was all I could do to mark a line on the paper where I was counting the number of trips.

After the first few minutes it actually became sort of pleasant. King was not crying or whining, he seemed really interested and excited in this weird thing we were doing, so there was no sound other than our feet pat-patting and our breathing, and I realized that we were actually engaged in a very complex dance. The feeling around this became stronger the longer I went without eye contact. The steps on the return trip to bed began to accumulate their own rhythm, and then there was my cover-smoothing, back-patting gesture, which ended our little dance sweetly. King, for his part, must have had his own rhythm: he lay in bed obediently until I left his bedroom, but as soon as I crossed the doorway and out of his sight, he must have hopped out of bed, because I would just get back to the table and have finished marking my line on the piece of paper where I was counting his trips in lines that I grouped into sets of five, when he was tap-tapping again, and I would turn to him (look at the wall) and we would start the dance over again.

After fifteen or twenty minutes passed—and it felt like we were really settled in our steps—I started wondering what King must be thinking of me: why isn't Mommy looking at me? Is something wrong? That's partly why I tried to make every touch I had with him—taking his hand, hoisting him on the bed, smoothing the covers, patting his back, just the two pats—very tender. I wanted the message to be, I love you, I am here, but we are not going to talk or play or giggle, it's time for sleep.

So he surprised me when, about half an hour into it,

instead of coming all the way out of the hallway into the light of the kitchen where I could see (though I chose not to) him, he kept his body in the shadows of the hallway and extended, into the light, his left hand, the one I had been taking in mine all these times. It was exactly like someone standing in the wings, extending their hand into a spotlight but keeping the rest of their body hidden. It was very Bob Fosse, actually.

It was moving to me because it showed how much he understood this strange thing we were doing: he knew that I was not looking at his face or body, but that I was permitting myself to look at his hand in order that I might hold it. His gesture not only said that he understood what I was doing, but that he wanted to take part in it, too—to withhold himself, as I was withholding my vision—and to present me with this smallified version of himself. He was withholding all view of himself except for his hand. It was such a beautiful mirroring gesture, and told me that he understood these strange rules we had cooked up and was willing to play along. This was all the more evident in the fact that the hand he presented to me, in that kitchen spotlight, was an open palm, reaching toward me as if to say, "here I am, a small me, the small me you are looking for, I wish you would see more, but if this is all you're going to see of me, here I am." It felt so brave and so loving on his part, actually much more loving than what we were doing in our stupid sleep training.

How often do people do this for others, I wonder, show the parts of themselves they know will be seen—no, reduce themselves to the parts they know the other person can or will see? Pretty often, I think. I think we do that all the time in families. Smallify ourselves to just a hand, if a hand is all that mommy or daddy can take.

8

Recently I had this idea, I wanted to get a scooter to zip around the city. In particular I had this idea that I want to drive King to school on the back of a scooter rather than take him in a cab or on the subway.

I started investigating, and it is a major pain, really, to get a scooter in New York City—if you want to get a fast one, that is. You can get the kind the delivery guys drive on the shoulder of the road and then you don't have to get a special license or anything, but you can only go 25 or 30 miles per hour, and I like my acceleration. So in order to get a scooter that actually has pickup—that can go, 60, say—you have to get a motorcycle license. And that entails first passing the written test at the DMV, and then passing the road test.

So I sent away for the motorcycle manual and studied it and then spent three hours at the DMV waiting to take the written test and then I took it and it was not hard: ten of the twenty questions were about drinking and driving and you don't have to be a genius to answer those. I got my permit and so did Frank and then our choice was either to get a bike and start riding around Manhattan without knowing what we were doing until we knew enough to take the road test, or take this thing called the Motorcycle Safety Foundation Basic Rider Skills Course, which is a three-day course, and at the end of it you take your road test with them and if you pass, you get a certificate and you can take it to the DMV and they give you your license on the spot. The course also provides you with bikes and helmets and all the other gear, so you don't have to buy anything first, which was good for us because we didn't have any of that stuff. We arranged to take the course, and have the boys hang out with Chandra.

I was excited about it. For the course you ride 250 cc motorcycles, which have a clutch lever on the left handlebar of the bike and a gearshift pedal by the left-foot peg. The scooter I wanted to buy didn't have any clutch lever or gearshift pedal, it's what they call a twist-n-go, and it basically operates like an automatic, with no shifting. I would just be learning all this shifting business to get my license. I had never driven anything but an automatic so the whole clutch thing had me a little worried, but I hoped I would be OK. It would be one three-hour evening of talking about motorcycles in a classroom and then one full day and one half day of riding motorcycles outside in a parking lot. So how bad could one full and one half day be?

8

There is this old idea that deep within a victimizer/victim relationship, there is an agreement, that each agrees on the arrangement. I think about that with my pedophile—why did I agree to that? Why did I agree to being raped and terrorized? Why didn't I tell someone? And on one hand I know why: because the pedophile scared me shitless and told me that if I told anyone about what he was doing, he would kill my family. And I believed him; I believed that in keeping quiet I was saving my family from death. I was very powerful for a four-year-old, really. In some ways I have never been as powerful as I was then.

8

I am imagining myself sailing down Ninth Avenue with my big-ass scooter going 65 miles per hour—what is the speed limit in New York City anyway? I think it's 35, but everyone knows that's fake. The speed limit is as fast as you can go, as fast as the traffic allows. The unwritten rule of traffic in New York City is that if there is a space ahead, you move into it.

I love New York City. I want to believe that in every new moment, everything is possible, and New York City helps me with that.

I have had the most astonishing cab rides in New York City. The whole thing feels like rolling the dice—who are you going to get? Who's going to be your driver? An angry driver can ruin the ride. I've had drunk drivers pick me up. One I remember, screaming down the Henry Hudson Parkway at 60 miles an hour, weaving between lanes, shouting something at me about the time he went to Jamaica and met a girl. I sat in the back and buckled my seatbelt and didn't say a word. I was younger then and afraid of everything, so when the things I really should have been afraid of happened, they were indistinguishable from all the regular fears I had all the time that I never acted on, so I didn't act on any fears, regular or not, and as a result I could not make myself safe at all.

I lived through that ride, and then there were other, better rides after that.

Not long ago I was in a cab with a driver, a young, good-looking black guy. He had an air about him—he seemed like a musician or a dancer. We were cruising slowly along West 11th Street, between Washington and the West Side Highway.

"Excuse me a minute," he said, and stopped the car in the middle of the block. Then he hopped out of the cab, leaving his door wide open, and stooped down in front of the vehicle so I couldn't see him anymore.

I was thinking what th-?

But then he stood up, hustled back into the cab, slammed the door, and then turned around and pushed a ten-dollar bill at me through the hole in the Plexiglas window. He pushed the bill at me in a very smooth, single-handed motion that allowed me to see that as he was pushing the bill, he was simultaneously pulling the bill off a very large stack of bills.

I knew without his having to say it in words that he had stopped the car because he had seen a wad of cash blowing across the street.

I laughed and said, "Oh my God!"

He was smiling but also seemed shaken up. He let out a

big breath as we turned onto the West Side Highway, into traffic.

"That's not the first time that's happened to me," he said softly.

We drove a little farther to my destination. My fare was five-something. To pay him, I gave him back the ten he had given me.

He turned around in his seat to face me as I pushed the bill through the window. I told him to keep the change.

"It feels good, doesn't it," he said, smiling.

I knew he meant giving—his giving and my giving and the whole shocking, giving universe.

I smiled a huge smile at him as I got out of the car.

There's no other way to put this, really: I loved him.

8

I went to see Vincent once every week or two. Sanghi wasn't sitting there tappity-tapping anymore. I would go in and sit down on his couch and tell him how things were going, and then I would lie on the massage table on my back and he would grasp my feet, and the way he grasped them reminded me of this time I saw a performance by Karen Finley, the infamous yam-stuffing artist. I was sitting in an almost front-row seat where I was able to see her standing in the wings, waiting to go on. I saw her standing in the dark, and then I saw the spotlight go on, and I saw her step into the spotlight. She stepped like a giant vertical praying mantis. She was standing very tall and still in the dark, and then she moved her whole body at once into the light, very quick and stiff on her two long back legs, with the praying legs hanging in front of her.

That's how Vincent grabbed my feet. He stood at the bottom of the table with his hands near my feet, not touching my feet, and then he moved so his two big hands were touching my feet, and the move was very fast, very intentional, and very charged.

He held my feet and the image I always had was that his arms were jumper cables, and I was a car.

And then at some point he would stop grasping my feet, and his hands would not be on my body at all, but the transition from grasping to not grasping was much less defined than the other way around—I barely had any knowledge of when or how he had stopped grasping my feet. I would just be lying there, daydreaming, and gradually over the course of the session I would become aware of where his hands were outside my body. Time would pass and all of a sudden I would think to myself, "Oh, I can feel his hands," and I would realize that I had been feeling his hands for maybe ten minutes, and in fact I knew exactly where they were outside my body even though they were not touching my skin.

I could feel this because he did something to the air between us that made it not ordinary air; it was very thick, and charged, but—and I must stress this because I know how it sounds—it was not sexual.

I was careful to observe it, and check: is it sexual? It was not.

He would end the session on my head, by which I mean his hands were over my head, maybe six inches over. One time, I remember, I could feel his hands over my head, and at the same time, inside my skull. I could actually feel the sensation of his hands on my brain although—I know this intellectually—my brain can't feel things, and his hands were not on my brain, they were not even on my body. Nonetheless, I felt him rubbing his fingers back and forth over my brain, like my brain was a nice wood coffee table he was rubbing with a cloth full of Pledge.

After that session, I could actually see colors brighter. It was unnerving. I felt like I had been wearing some kind of veil that he had rubbed off. I found myself feeling more sensitive to people. As I left his apartment I was in the elevator with a guy who was clearly on a lot of medication and I felt like his whole body was surrounded by a buzzing, clear black cloud. The guy himself did not scare me, but the cloud did.

I felt like I was missing some armor. The next time I came into see Vincent I asked him not to clean my brain again. We laughed about it. He said OK, though.

I only saw Vincent for a couple months and then he moved to Portland. He told me he'd keep me posted as to when he was coming back into town.

I was sad when he left; I felt really good when I went to him. It was a similar feeling to when you go swimming in the ocean and then lie in the sun for a few minutes. Every time I ended a session I felt like my eyes were bigger in my head, like a baby. I was softer and more relaxed. Plus, I got to lie there and feel his not-on-my-body, in-the-air hands, and feel where they were, and think if I can feel them, and they're not on me, and they're in space, then what is it, after all, that separates people? I have heard this before: what separates people isn't distance, it's time.

8

If you really and truly want to have new and different
things happen in your life, it is good if you can spend time
trying to be open to them. You would be surprised at how
hard it is to be open to new and different good things.
Being open to new things that are bad—disasters, say—is
pretty easy. There are a lot of images floating around to
help. But new, good things are a challenge.

Here is a simple exercise:

   —Sit down.

   —Think of the most spectacularly wonderful thing
      you can ever imagine. If it means you are naked
      rolling around having sex with forty people on a
      mountain of gold doubloons, then fine. Spend a
      lot of time imagining that, get a lot of details.
      When it is really clear, when you have the whole
      thing spread out in front of you like a giant field
      of daisies and if you wanted you could reach out
      and pick one, try to feel what it would feel like for
      something even more spectacularly wonderful
      than that to suddenly show up for you.

It's hard, isn't it? I can't really do it. I start at the part where

I try to think of the most spectacularly wonderful thing I can ever imagine, and then I just end up thinking about sex, which is good, I guess, but hardly new. In fact, I usually end up thinking about sex that has already happened.

It's really difficult to overstate how hard it is for most grown people to imagine anything new, and how much easier it is to not imagine at all, but to really feel, to really believe, that disasters they have already experienced are bound to happen again.

8

I'm coming back here again now, into this book, after I thought I had finished it, and Grave Digger is my inspiration, and as we all know, an inspiration is a motivator, it is something that acts as a catalyst, it allows one to do what one would not otherwise be able to do. So now I will attempt to do what I should have done before, which is to provide you with a clear and understandable explanation of biodynamic craniosacral therapy (biodynamic CST). You haven't been introduced to biodynamic CST yet, but it is coming soon. I realized after I thought I had finished this that I shirked it—it meaning biodynamic CST—I brought it up but then I didn't follow it through completely. I talked about what I found on the web and I complained about how it wasn't very informative, but then I didn't offer anything else. In my (weak) defense I will say that I thought you had to be an expert to try and explain it and I am not an expert. But now I see that that isn't the most important thing. The most important thing is remembering Grave Digger.

I will explain the mechanics of biodynamic CST in a minute. But first I must tell you that explaining the mechanics, while helpful, doesn't explain what it is— at least not to me. I can't robot-explain it because my real understanding of biodynamic CST is not through my brain, or even through words that are direct and comprehensible. My understanding of it comes through what I have experienced with my body, as a client, and through casual conversations I have had with Patricia Codrington, the biodynamic craniosacral therapist I have been fortunate enough to work with for over a year now.

I have tried to talk to Patricia many times about what exactly she is doing when I lay down on her table and she places her hand under the small of my back. She never gives me a straight answer. This is not because she is being evasive, I think, but because a straight answer does not exist. I think what she does when she touches my body is access something that is like time. It might actually be time, I am not sure. If it is, it is time in the way I talked about it in the beginning of this book—time as a plastic medium that surrounds us and that is in every cell of our bodies—and not time like tick tick. She is holding the body in time and within that—"that" meaning time as a space—she is holding all that has happened and all that has the potential to happen. She is holding me not only as bones and sinew that was organized in a certain way—although certainly there is no escaping that—but also as a potency.

The mechanics are helpful to know, though, so let me review them with you: in craniosacral therapy, the therapist touches the client's body in order to assess the craniosacral system, which is a circulatory system that includes the skull, spine, sacrum, meninges, cerebrospinal fluid, and brain. The craniosacral system, like the heart-oriented circulatory system, has a pulse. Practitioners disagree on the rate of the pulse, but Patricia says she likes to work with it at four cycles per minute.

In biodynamic CST, which is the type of CST I will be focused on here, the therapist touches the body in order to make contact with the (unfortunately

named, in my view) Breath of Life. The Breath of
Life, which was discovered and named by a very
brave and interesting American osteopath named
William Sutherland, exists invisibly in and around the
cerebrospinal fluid. It is often described as an inher-
ent force, similar to prana or chi, that is with a person from the moment of conception until death, and
that acts as a blueprint for the body's development.
This is why a biodynamic craniosacral therapist
working with your body may be able to tell you
about something that happened to you in utero.

Craniosacral therapy, whether biodynamic or any
other kind, is usually not taken seriously by many
western doctors not only because of the difficulty in
discussing palpation, but because one of the funda-
mental tenets of the craniosacral system model is that
the bones of the skull articulate: the edges of the
skull bones are beveled, and move slightly according
to the rhythms and fluctuations of the cerebrospinal
fluid.

The current theory among most traditional western
doctors, however, is that the skull bones fuse in childhood and then sit in your head, for the rest of your
life, like a big upside-down bowl at the top of your
body.

8

A little over a year ago King had fluid in his ears. It sat there and sat there and there wasn't a ton of it and it wasn't infected and it didn't warrant antibiotics but still it sat there. King's pediatrician finally said, "I'll give you the number of a craniosacral therapist, maybe she can get it to drain." She told me her name, Patricia Codrington.

Our pediatrician is excellent in all the traditional ways, but she is also open to alternative healing methods.

"She's a little out there," the doctor warned me.

I didn't tell her I had already been out there myself, with Vincent.

"No problem," I said.

8

I started my motorcycle course, and I'm freaking exhausted. Last night we sat in class for three hours and read the course manual and answered questions from the back of the manual. We talked about motorcycles and how to drive them and how to ride them. Then before we went home we all sat at our desks with our feet flat on the floor and

our arms out in front of us, and pretended we were grip-
ping the motorcycle handlebars. Then we pretended to
turn the ignition (right hand), squeeze the clutch (left
hand), put the bike in neutral (left foot), accelerate (right
hand), and release the clutch (left hand). It was a nice way
to end the evening, with all of us tapping on the floor with
our feet and holding our arms out in front of us like zombies, wiggling our balled-up hands on our wrists.

But today the riding was for real, and Frank and I got there
at 9 a.m. because we were supposed to get there at 9:30,
and then we found out class wasn't going to start until 11.
We sat and studied the questions in the back of the manual for a long time, and then finally the instructor came
and helped us finish the questions and then we took the
written test and I am happy to say I got 100 percent cor-
rect; yay, I am a good motorcycle student, sitting at my
desk in the nice, warm classroom.

There was one line from the manual in particular that I
loved, from the introduction to the section about dogs
who like to chase motorcycles. I highlighted it:

> We live in an imperfect world. Sometimes factors
> develop and interact in subtle ways.

8

Patricia Codrington is a solid fifty-something lady who was born in Trinidad and raised in Tobago. She has a big, easy smile and a relaxed, no-bullshit manner. She is a family nurse practitioner, and you can easily imagine her doing the work she used to do before she hung out her craniosacral shingle, which was tending to patients immediately after they came out of open-heart surgery, in a cardiac unit in a hospital.

I took King to see her. I watched as she put him on the sheet-covered massage table and sat next to the table on a big blue exercise ball and held his ankles. I didn't question why she was holding his ankles when I have to say I assumed she would be holding his head, considering I thought this craniosacral business was supposed to be about the brain and spinal cord. I guess I have Vincent to thank for this, that the foot no longer seems weird to me as an entry point.

King seemed fine. He was sitting there, eating animal crackers as she held his ankles. Then he lay down, and started to cry, and tried to crawl away, but it was hard to tell if this was from something Patricia was doing or just because he was three.

We managed to keep him on the table for a few more minutes with toys and snacks, and at the end of the session

Patricia told me King had some kind of bone jamming in his skull, she used the bone names: the occiput and the something. I was concerned, of course, to hear about this, and I asked her how serious it was.

She held her hand out toward me. "Do you want to feel it?" she asked.

"Yes," I said, looking at her, I think, with a little dread.

She took my right hand, and I felt something traveling up my arm, to the base of my skull on the right side, where it stopped, and then I felt a dull, hard pain there.

I took my hand out of hers quickly, as if she had burned me, and asked her, "Is he in pain?"

"No," she said, calmly, returning her hand to her side, "every body is different."

8

In motorcycle safety class we actually talked a lot about time and space because it is constantly hammered in your head in class that time *is* space. When you ride your motorcycle you are supposed to have a space cushion around you at all times. How big should the space cushion be? Two seconds big, because two seconds is the minimum amount of time it will take you to react to something. How do you know how big two seconds of space is? It's actually an easy formula—you wait until the car ahead of you passes a sign, and then you count onemotorcycle, twomotorcycle, and if you reach the sign at the same time you say twomotorcycle there is a space cushion between you and the car that is two seconds big.

I loved talking about that, but then I also loved how right before we finally went out to the parking lot to get on the bikes for the first time, our fabulous instructor, Antonio, told us to stop thinking.

"You have to feel it," he said.

8

After King's first appointment with Patricia I made one for myself. She had me lay on my back on the table and then she held her hand under the small of my back rather than holding me by the ankles. I lay there for about forty-five minutes. It was not at all like Vincent and the jumper cables. She did not make the air around my body thick and furry, and she did not blur the line where my body ended and other bodies began.

She made my body feel like an effervescent tablet that had

just been submerged in water. I felt like all these bubbles were streaming up off of me, into the air, making me lighter and freer as they went. The closest thing I have ever had to this sensation is the few times I have spent intensely praying, when I have had a very slight sense that something is streaming up and off my head and shoulders.

After this first appointment with Patricia I made another one, and then another. At this time—about nine months ago—I was aware of the pedophile, I knew that it had happened, I had the memories, but it was far away. Not far away like long ago, though. It was not like the story of my life was a straight line trailing behind me like a tail, with one event after another, some closer to me and some farther away. It was like the story of my life was not attached to me at all, it was a globe on a library table somewhere, and the pedophile was down on the bottom of the globe in a white and black blob like Antarctica. Not a place you really go unless you're doing research.

On my fifth or sixth appointment with Patricia I was lying on my back on the table as usual and Patricia had her left hand under the small of my back as usual and then she put her right hand over my right hip bone and she said, "There's some trauma there. Do you want to release it?"

It seemed so unbelievable to me that she said that: do I want to release it? I have been in therapy for twenty years talking about my trauma-induced problems, trying to talk them out, trying to purge them, trying to move up and on and over to a place with no or less or reduced amount of problems, trying to let go of these problems that seemed to be like a big mass of poop glued to my hands, and there I was standing at the cliff's edge shaking my poop-covered hands, trying to throw my problems away, to get them off me, and instead all that happened was that more crap flew by and this mound of crap/problems glued to my hands was not falling into the abyss at all, it was gradually getting bigger and heavier, and shaking it was proving to be harder and harder, until at last I could hardly hold my hands up to shake them at all. Do I want to release it?

I laughed. "Yeah," I said.

"You might relive it a little here," she said, meaning there, on the table.

"It's OK," I said. I figured the trauma was the pedophile, but it didn't bother me. I had lived though it already.

So she put her hand there again, and I felt the streaming up from that area, a warmth, and that was all.

The session was over a few minutes later. I sat in the waiting room and put on my boots.

"You might have some memories and things," she said again.

"It's OK," I said. I wasn't sure whether I believed her or not.

Two days later it was like I found myself alone in a small art gallery, where a tiny black-and-white image I had previously glanced at only on a contact sheet full of other tiny images was now on display in front of me, under gallery lighting, as a glorious five- by six-foot color print. The image was of me, floating on the ceiling of my bedroom in Connecticut late at night after the pedophile tried to rape me. I was up there until very early in the morning when two strangers—whose exact features I don't remember, I recall only that they were exceedingly nice and seemed like twins—came to visit me, and we hung out and they said very nice things to me that made me feel better, but they also kept telling me that I had to go back into my body and I kept telling them that I didn't want to go.

In the end I did what I was told, though; I went back down into my body, which sucked, I remember, just as I thought it would. And as I went down, they left, and I was all alone in my room.

Then later in the morning Mrs. Dauth came in and got me and she drove me to a doctor without speaking about what we were doing or where we were going, and I said nothing, and when I was on the examination table I said nothing, just looked at the doctor, who looked at my private parts and said I would be OK, and Mrs. Dauth said something about how it had happened that was a lie, and I heard her lie, and said nothing; I said nothing the entire time. I was doing something inside myself that is hard to put into words. It was taking all my energy. I was very full, I was very powerful, I was gigantic with the fullness and power with which I was watching everyone do everything.

8

In motorcycling today, I learned that when you go faster, things are smoother. It's a smoother ride, if you are going very fast, than if you go slow. If you go slow, you feel every little bump.

I had to keep telling myself to relax my shoulders, I was driving the bike like Frankenstein. When I relaxed it was much easier to steer.

I was just on this little Kawasaki 150, basically a dirtbike, in a parking lot in Queens. The more experienced riders— Frank was one—got to ride 250s, but not me. This was my first time ever on a motorcycle, as a driver.

The instructors had to keep telling me to keep my eyes up and look through the turns. It was weird how that one kicked in—it really is true—where you look, you go. Where you look, the bike follows. It's like having a robot attached to you.

This is different than a car, of course. In a car you are your same self, driving your car with its little details that speak of you. On a bike you are not your same self; you are a biker. You are a man or woman attached to a bike, you are a new form, and the biggest factor about you—they tell you this over and over in motorcycle safety school—is that cars do not see you. Even when you are at intersections and thinking you are making eye contact with the car-drivers, you should not assume they see you. You are invisible. They are not expecting to see you, and on some level maybe they don't really even want to see you, because you are small and fast and annoying and they don't know what to do with you.

8

I recently found out my mom also had a pedophile. I found out because my mom emailed me during this period when this memory of the pedophile was very present and she asked me how I was doing, and I just didn't have the energy to make it all nice for her. My mom already knows about the pedophile, I told her and my father almost twenty years ago, when I quit drinking and the memories of it first came. And they responded to it like I guess you would expect—they were horrified. They sat there and were horrified at a restaurant where we ate lunch and I told them, and then we finished lunch and we didn't talk about it too much after that.

My dad passed away several years ago. So when my mom e-mailed me and asked me how I was, I wrote her that I was not great, that I was having some memories of Mr. Dauth but otherwise everything was fine. I didn't delve into it, didn't make it all emotional, I just included it as a fact in an email.

She wrote me back:

> I am sorry to learn that you are still having problems with past experiences . . . with Mr. Dauth. I only wish that somehow Mr. Dauth will rot in hell for what he did to you. You must put all that behind you . . . for there is so much you need to do now

for your little, wonderful boys and for Frank. The world is full of Dauthlike crazies . . . so protect your sons from similar situations, watching over them as much as you can. Be aware of everyone. I mean, everyone!

I have never told anyone of some of the experiences I had as a child, and I know the problems that can come about as a result of it, but you just have to be strong and not let it get to you. You were not at fault. It was not your fault! If anything, it was mine! For going off on a vacation and leaving you with a babysitter. But, how was I to know that HE would take advantage of this situation. So, this is why I say, be aware of everyone.

I wrote her back saying I was very grateful she had told me that, and that I would really love hearing anything else she felt comfortable telling me about her experiences as a child, that I thought it would help me.

She wrote me and said she didn't want to tell me anything else.

This was last year and we haven't spoken of it since.

8

When an event happens, you carry it. These events you

carry have power. They work like magnets, only instead of attracting their opposites they attract things like themselves.

The older you get the more you are actually like a very imposing tribal chief wearing a hundred thousand event-amulets around your neck. These amulets sit and stir on your chest like a tornado, and suck things toward you, from the future.

To put it another way: the past has a force, and its force contributes to your velocity as you are riding along on the teeny tiny point of time called the present. You would not believe how much force you have running through you in the present. You get up, you brush your teeth, you think another day, another dollar, and you forget that you are wearing a breastplate of bloody jewels and bones, and the past is whorling around your heart and the future is rushing toward you, and you are standing there, whitening your teeth and combing your wig—you are alive, really, you are—and it is like you are riding a unicycle on a high wire at 100 miles an hour over a canyon.

You can see, then, given your precarious position as a human being, how important your every little action is.

8

After three grueling hours of motorcycle practice yesterday morning in freezing-cold Queens, I took my motorcycle road test and flunked it. There were four parts to the
test: U-turns, swerving, braking, and curving. Apparently
the problem was that I did not accelerate enough in my
swerving and curving. I don't know, I thought I was doing
OK, I actually liked swerving when we were practicing it
on the lot today, it reminded me a lot of skating.
Motorcycling itself reminds me a lot of skating. There is
the whole feeling of gliding—of leaning and flow. The first
part of the test—the U-turns—was basically exactly like a
figure skating test, only on a motorcycle. We had to do a
figure 8 on the bike, but a very tight, controlled figure 8,
where we had to stay within the marked-off boundaries of
a long, narrow patch of parking lot. Everybody in class was
having a hard time with it, wobbling outside the desig-
nated space or putting a foot down for balance. People
were getting nervous as they were practicing, worried that
they would fail the test because they couldn't do the 8, but
the instructors told them that it was weighted the least on
the test, and not to worry about it.

I did OK on the figure 8. But it was the swerving, curving, and accelerating that were important, and I choked on
those. I know I am a good rider. Somehow when it came
to the test I just got all spooked and tentative.

I was so frustrated when I found out I flunked that I almost started crying right there with Gary, the head teacher, beside me. I think everyone else in class passed but me.

After the test I felt like such a loser, I hated motorcycles, I hated everything to do with motorcycles—the smell and the colors and the oils and liquids and revving and vibrating and smoke and chains clanking, it was all ghouls, it was all zombies rattling around. I am supposed to get one free retest for the course—I am scheduled to come back to do it next weekend—but if I don't pass after that, I am screwed.

If I don't pass the retest I never want to talk about this idea of riding motorcycles and loving my robot-self ever again. I just want to live not being a robot, with my feet on the earth, on a farm with no machines, where we plow the field with spoons and eat chunky applesauce and that's all.

Frank had to work yesterday, so he didn't take his test yet. We are scheduled to go back to Queens together.

Frank says he is proud of me and he gave me a big hug and that helps but it still sucks.

8

Last night, the night after the morning I failed my motor-cycle test, I was up with a cough. By that I mean not that I woke up and coughed, I mean that a cough woke me up. This never happens to me—my body never wakes me up while I am sleeping, my body is so ecstatic to be sleeping that it sleeps deep, wonderful sleep that it is wrenched from only by small boys. So to be woken up by my own body felt like: what is happening? Why is my body both-ering me? Doesn't it know who is boss here?

I coughed so hard I was crying. The cough felt like a big, heavy spider's web trembling in my chest. I went rummag-ing in the medicine cabinet to see if we had any syrup of any kind, and we had one unopened bottle of something but it felt too hard to turn on the light and read the bot-tle so I didn't, I just took three tiny sips of it in the dark and hoped that it wasn't the kind of medicine that was going to keep me up.

After that I sat up in bed with pillows propped behind me because it seemed like sitting up was better than lying down, as far as coughing went, and I sucked on a honey lemon cough drop I found by moving my hand around in a drawer like a squirrel, and I realized that this is how my mother sleeps now, as an old woman: she sits propped up sucking a cough drop, perfectly still except for the little sucking motions of her mouth. She sleeps like this because she has a cough, which she inherited from my grandmother, who also had a cough and who also slept, since the time she had her accident, sitting up. Her accident happened a few months before I was born. She drove her car across a railroad track and into an oncoming train. She lost her left leg—it was amputated at mid-thigh, and her husband, my grandfather, who was riding in the front passenger seat. He died.

The grandmother-mother cough is mysterious. My grandmother went to a bunch of doctors, who couldn't figure out what it was. My mom also went to a bunch of doctors, who said it might be asthma, but they weren't sure. Both my grandmother and my mom ended up combating their coughs with minty things to suck on. In my grandmother's case it was Starlite mints. My mother's remedy is less sweet: mentholyptus cough drops.

I was propped up, coughing, feeling like my mom and my grandma, thinking thoughts, with something in my mouth.

I was not like my mom or my grandma, though, in that I was all sad and crabby about failing my motorcycle test.

I felt in my coughing and crying that I was having a grief. It was like I had a cold—I had a grief. It was like my body was waking me up, tapping me on the shoulder to cry out some thing I couldn't or wouldn't know.

I coughed and cried sitting up in the middle of the night and I thought: this has to be about something bigger than a motorcycle test, what is it?

My brain wasn't coming up with anything. So I sat there with my body like my body was one of my sons, lying on me crying as they sometimes do. I sat there and let this heavy, wet, spasm-y thing do its thing.

There was a little space between us, my body and me. It struck me then that this was the opposite of what I had been trying so hard to do all day in the parking lot, which was to make the motorcycle an extension of me. In class I was in my body and trying to make the motorcycle another part of my body and it was day and sunny and I was cold and shivering and all too aware of my body. Now it was night and I was at home, warm in bed, and not even attached to my body myself.

I started thinking maybe I am going about things the wrong way. Maybe this idea of making the motorcycle an extension of my body is wrong. Maybe my body doesn't want a motorcycle attached to it. Maybe my body doesn't want to be a part-robot.

And then I thought of my grandmother and how she had the prosthetic leg she had to learn to walk with, and how hard that must have been and maybe she was humiliated about it—a grown woman having to learn to walk again. Maybe she didn't think it was cute and funny at all, the way my mother always told me the story, that grandma learned to walk with her granddaughter. Maybe she didn't like her big, expensive fake leg. Maybe she hated her new, dumb life with a big fake leg and no husband. Maybe she wished she had killed herself in that car, too.

8

King goes to sleep in his bed on his own without a problem now. I don't know how it happened. It wasn't the sleep training. We stopped doing that a little while after we started. I think we just kept saying go back to bed until finally the novelty of getting out of bed wore off.

We had the opposite experience with Mick: he learned how to crawl out of his crib shortly before his second birthday, and we suffered for at least two months, having him come into our bed and sleep/kick us all night long, and we slogged through like this because we were too tired to put him back into the crib, and because sometimes even if we did muster the energy to put him back, he would still climb back out and come into bed with us. So we went on like this, in no rush to get him a bed because we figured if he gets out of the crib of course he will get out of the bed.

But it turns out that Mick really just wanted a bed. The night we got him his twin bed he slept in it all night and never got out. And he is still like that three months later.

The issue now is that he wants me to lie in bed with him until he falls asleep. If I don't lie there, he climbs out of bed and finds me and says "Mommy, come," and holds my hand and leads me back to his bed. It's exactly what I was doing with King's sleep training, only opposite.

Here is how I approach the sleep problem now: I muddle through it, and I say it will not last forever.

8

I should know something about what it means to be touched, having had a pedophile. I know from my own experience that what I was doing—sucking the pedophile's dick, for instance, in a parking lot near ballet class—was not, I don't want to say damaging, but let's say, that wasn't the part that fazed me. I didn't know that what the pedophile and I were doing was sex because I didn't know what sex was. I knew that what he was doing was weird and fierce, but it wasn't that horrible. The more horrible part was how he terrified me. The touching was not a big deal compared to that. So I of anyone should know that touch is not all that. It is not the end-all and be-all, the big, scary thing, like putting a key in someone. It doesn't unlock them.

I remember now hearing a woman at a party who said that once she was drunk on the subway and there was a nun in her subway car, and she went over and asked the nun why she believed in God, and the nun said, "Because there is a place inside me that no one can touch."

I believe that. I know that to be true, myself.

I have asked Patricia several times to explain to me what she is doing when she holds King. Once she went so far as to tell me that she was touching him with a sensitivity she has built up over time, but then she got almost vehement about it: "You can't explain the touch, you can't explain the touch," she said.

Patricia is supposed to be working on the writing for her web site now. I said I would help her with it. So I went in to see Patricia myself today, and I asked her: What are you going to do about your web site? Are you going to talk about your touch? I had already complained to her about how I think craniosacral therapy looks like crap on the web, how anyone trying to find anything about it can't find anything at all that explains things in a coherent way. John Upledger, a CST pioneer based in Florida whose

CST workshops can be found all over the world, goes so far as to say on his site that "using a soft touch," therapists "release restrictions," but he doesn't explain how that happens. He does list the ailments that CST is helpful in treating, though—it is nineteen entries long and ranges from migraine headaches to colic.

Which is fabulous, of course. Who wants to quibble with something that is possibly effective against colic? But my question was—still is—what are practitioners doing with their soft touch?

I told this to Patricia and she said she was going to say something about how biodynamic craniosacral therapy is about "making contact with biodynamic processes," and I asked her what biodynamic processes were and she didn't answer, but instead she cut me off and said it's not about how you talk about craniosacral therapy it's about how you hear it.

Then she asked me: "What comes up for you when you hear about the therapy, what issues come up for you that keep you from believing that it is possible to be touched?"

When I heard that I could see Frank rolling his eyes like he does when anyone talks about astrology.

After my session was over she came back to the subject.

"Craniosacral therapy is making contact with a human being that goes beyond an ordinary understanding of 'laying of hands'—it's really making contact, palpation—thereby the human being is found," she said.

"You're saying that a human being is more than the body, then," I said.

She thought for a second, and then said, "You probably need to consider what a human being is, too."

I put my boots on. I was thinking about human beings as bodies, and how we are all walking around sweating and smelling with our heavy footsteps and our disgusting excretions, and how occasionally we lie down and groan and let another body out, and how insane that is, and how hard it is to propel your body somewhere, and what a pain it is that you have to get into an airplane to fly, and how the body needs to be wiped and cleaned and bathed and dried and watered and fed and emptied and watered again, over and over a gazillion times, and still it breaks down anyway.

And then I was thinking, well, that's one thing. But there is more to a person than that.

8

Another cab ride:

I got into the cab and told the driver where I wanted to go, and as I told him I glanced at him—he was wearing a tie and a coat and a chauffeur's hat. I don't have to tell you that drivers of taxis in New York City don't usually dress up like this.

Just in case I missed it, he called my attention to his outfit.

"Bet you don't see a driver like this everyday," he said.

Sometimes the crazy drivers really want to talk and once they get started you can't stop them.

"No," I said.

He told me he liked to dress up for his job. Then he showed me his tie, which had an American flag motif on it. He had worn this tie every day since September 11, he said.

I thought I might as well dive into it.

"Where were you that day?" I asked.

He didn't tell me, exactly. He was a chauffeur, he said. But after September 11 he decided to drive a cab, only he still wore his chauffeur's outfit.

"That's great," I said.

He said he wanted to dress properly for his job; he wanted to provide me with a positive experience. He wanted me to leave his cab in a more positive frame of mind than when I entered it. I should think of him as a computer icon, he said, and whenever I was feeling negative, I should think of him, my positive taxi driver, and feel the positive feelings he wanted me to have.

"That's beautiful," I said.

He continued talking about himself and his positivity and how important it was to be positive and as he was talking— his voice was almost a monotone, it was actually slightly robotic—I was thinking he seemed to have that single-mindedness of someone who has endured a trauma, of someone who is stuck somewhere and the somewhere is not exactly here and now. And then I looked at the back of his head and noticed his coloring—he was pale to such a degree that he seemed to be almost albino, and suddenly I had this intense fear that my taxi driver was not in fact alive, that he was the ghost of someone who had died on 9/11 and was trying to come back to help, and as I listened to him go on about his positivity, and his outfit, and his tie, and his cab, and his being a computer icon, and his hope and desire for all good things for me, I looked at his license and saw the name

HINTERSTEINER
PAUL

in plain black letters and I felt the possibility that everything around me, building after building, street after street, was not in fact a thing after thing I was sailing safely past in my for-a-moment taxi, but that the whole thing—the taxi, the streets, the buildings, the entire city of New York itself—was some kind of black velvet bag I was swinging in, and who was the holding the bag? And as we started rounding the corners of Washington Square Park, I said, "here," and on the southwest corner he pulled over and the meter started making its chinking sound and spit out the paper receipt from its slot, and then I gave him money and he gave me money back, and then he gave me something else: a piece of paper with a picture of a swan on it, and the following words:

Are you Surprised to see **Dressed Up Taxi Driver**? I use to be a Limo Driver before 9/11. I traded my Black Car in for a Yellow Car. (Before 9/11 in February of 2001 the bubble busted on the Dot Com's, then millions of millions of people was laid off all over the world. Then all the businesses cut all there expense accounts to zero. A ripple effect happen, and all the businesses that supported the other businesses, then they laid off and some went bust. Then when the World Trade Center got hit. It just put the Icing on the Cake, and it blow everything out of the ballpark for everybody.) So I am still chauffeuring people around. Why shouldn't I dress **Appropriately**, **Positively**, and **Professionally**. Because I want you to leave my car more **Positive** then you came in and have a more **Positive Day** (Weekend, Flight, stay in New York City, etc.)

Any time you have any **Negativity**, picture me as a **Computer Icon** in your **Mind**. As the only Taxi Driver wearing a chauffeurs uniform, and a **American Flag Tie**, (since 9/11) and listens to **Classical Music** everything is **Positive and Relaxing**. So any time you have any **Negativity** you pull up my **Icon and double click on it**, and let my **Positiveity** flow out so to get rid of the Negativity getting in, use me as a **Catalyst** to get you started. Everybody needs help? So I planted the **Seed** of **Positiveity** in your **Subconscious Mind**. So any time you need me I will be their to **Help** you and **Support** you. **Just think of me**.

8

I have been trying to think if anything new and different has ever happened in my life, and I can't really come up with anything. I guess my standards are high. I am not talking about buying a new sweater. I am not even talking about riding around with Hintersteiner Paul. I am talking about something mind-blowingly new, where you suddenly find yourself in a new and different environment with new and different rules, where you don't recognize anything but it's not like a disaster, it's the most wonderful and beautiful thing that's ever happened to you and you are not scared.

I don't think anything like that has ever happened to me. Maybe it's impossible for anything like that to happen unless you are on drugs or dying. Maybe the yearning for it is not meant to be fulfilled; maybe it's just some kind of built-in spiritual longing.

I don't think that anything new and different has ever happened in my life, but something interesting did. I am not talking about the pedophile now. I am done talking about the pedophile like it's interesting. This happened around the same time as the pedophile, though, when I was four.

My mom took me to a theater in Connecticut, to a performance of Sleeping Beauty. We had seats at the end of the row, next to the center aisle. My seat was at the very end of the row, next to the aisle, and my mother's seat was next to me. We were just a few rows from the stage. When I looked straight down the aisle I saw a short stairway, four wooden steps, that connected the floor of the theater to the floor of the stage.

I spent the bulk of the performance studying these steps. The steps were there. They existed. Therefore, I reasoned, it was possible, it was even sanctioned, that people should sometimes move from the floor of the theater, where my feet were not quite touching as I sat in my cushy red chair, to the floor of the stage.

As the play went on, I moved forward in my seat. I was still studying the stairs. I wanted to go up the stairs. I wanted to break into that space. I wanted to go from the dark no-talking space to the bright talking space. I wanted to go from the place with mothers and chairs to the place with queens and princes and evil people who were recognized as such.

At last Sleeping Beauty was poisoned. She was sleeping it off on the beautiful bed and the prince came onstage and came upon her and was very sad. He wanted to kiss her, he said.

"I can show you how to kiss," I said, as I ran up the steps into his lap.

This was community theater. Up-close the prince seemed very old, with jarring orange makeup on. I sat in his lap. His head and neck drew back in a way that was snakelike. But then he came forward again, and smiled.

He was so grateful that I had come to show him how to kiss, he said. He wasn't sure he knew how to do it.

We kissed several times, to make sure he got it right.

I was happy to help him. My heart was big, as King sometimes says when he is happy.

I remember looking down at Sleeping Beauty, who also looked very unappealing and orange up-close. She was smiling with her eyes closed.

Eventually she was awakened and I had to go down the steps and back into my chair but I don't remember that part.

When I think about this event now I think how amazing it is that my mother did not stop me—that she did not run after me or yell at me to come down or scold me afterwards or wring her hands that I was some kind of social misfit or take me to a pediatric neurologist because I seemingly could not tell theater from life. She was proud, I remember. We left the theater and she walked beside me and I knew she was happy and now when I think about that I think, thank God. Thank you, Mom.

8

I have been told by the editor at the publishing company that has agreed to publish this, the editor whose name is also Amy, and who I have been calling Ate, for Amy-the-editor, in emails to certain friends, that this section you have just finished reading is not believable.

"Are you sure it wasn't a dream?" she asked me gently as I sat across the table from her in her publishing company office.

She went on to say that she had submitted this manuscript to some students she had had in a publishing course earlier in the summer, and this was what kept coming up for the students: they didn't believe this part.

I was pretty much on autopilot at this meeting, so I

dealt with the subject at hand without any added emotion. I told Ate that my mother had been with me and would testify to the event's truth, and that my neighbor-friend from childhood had heard about the event and had drawn a picture of me kissing the prince, which she presented to me one day when I was playing at her house, and that I believed the picture had macaroni on it.

Ate suggested that I include those details.

What I could not say at the time, and what I want to say now—now, again, meaning later—is that this is a problem for us, and by "us" I mean not only me and Ate, but me and Ate and you, you meaning the reader, and even people who do not read this book, people who do not read because they don't like books like this or because they are too busy with small children, or even people who do not read at all, people like the small children themselves, because it is this "us," editors and writers and readers and non-readers, this "us" of society, who have to come to some agreement of what "real" is.

And of course what I am getting at here is the old idea that what is "real" is a construct we have decided upon, and that children getting raped is part of this realness: it is "real" but most likely not real in that it does not happen to you or even someone you know. At least I hope not. The way children getting raped is "real" for most people is that they see women on TV talking about it or read women in magazines talking about it, or hear men in the news, say, in a court-room, like in the Boston church scandal, talking about it—very quick there, just a word or two—or hear reporters on the news talking about it without the rapee's voice in it at all. These are all adults talking. And with the exception of the TV news reporters—who presumably have not been raped as children, but really, who can tell—these adults who are in the media in one way or another talking about being raped are talking about it as if it is still happening. They are talking about it as if they are still being victimized by it, even though it is not happening in their lives at this moment, it has long passed.

But this is the way we are used to seeing it. We see child rape presented as grown-ups talking and crying. It's like seeing a time-warp, all these grown-ups stuck in this time-bubble talking about the same thing. We don't see children on TV or on talk shows saying "I was raped," and I am assuming there is some idea behind this about protecting the children, because it's always about protecting the fucking children, but it also seems clear that what is also being protected is our version of what child rape is, which is adults— and mostly lady adults, thank you very much—crying in their time warp on TV, because ladies do a lot of that. Men, not so much.

Female adults crying is an OK-way to hear about children being raped, we have agreed on that. It is really not OK to have a woman go on TV and say "Motherfucker raped me up the ass!" and to pump her fist in the air and to talk about how great her life is, and her sex life is, and her family is, to talk like "thank you rapist," thank you in that whatever-does-not-kill-me-makes-me-stronger-way. And this is understandable, it's just a social need; we can't really go around thanking rapists when we are also supposedly trying so hard to put them in jail.

What the adult women on TV or in magazines are allowed to say is pretty limited, it seems. You generally don't hear much beyond the it-wasn't-supposed-to-happen/it-happened dichotomy, which is where the time warp operates, because to move past a trauma it is necessary to accept that it happened, and both the women speaking and the people watching—i.e., us— seem to have a hard time accepting that, which is, again, understandable: child rape is horrific act. Who wants to accept that it happens? But the tenacity with which we hold onto the idea that it is not supposed to happen reflects, I think, the power of another "real" story we have told ourselves, which is the story of what childhood is.

Childhood, the story goes, is not a time, it's a place. It is a place that is within our adult time/place, but not of it. It is like a soap bubble floating around in the "real" world, and in this rainbow-colored soap bubble, which we adults believe we work very hard to protect, the children reside, and they are allowed to be insane in there, by which I mean they are allowed to be really fucking creative, to give a voice and history and name to every single object they touch, to make something—Jupiter—out of something else—a dish-scrubber—hundreds and hundreds of times a day. And we adults protect this rainbow-colored bubble, the idea goes, as long as we possibly can, although if I were to continue this rant in as many digressions as I would like to, I would add that what we really do is drum this fantastic ability out of our children so that we are sure that by the time they are in high school they will be too scared to try anything "creative" unless they have already been told repeatedly by many grown-ups that they are "good" at it.

And without going too far astray, what I mean here is that we do this thing where we make "art class," in which we work with glue and paint and make pictures of things that there is increasing pressure, in early childhood, to name—this is a house; this is a tree; this is not a picture of how I can visit all fifty states at once—and slowly this idea is born that art is a subject that requires certain materials and is separate from other subjects like "reading" and "math." And then we introduce music and maybe theater as other "arts," and although it is understandable that these things should be introduced this way, it is still here in this categorization of what "being creative" is and where we can "be creative,"—with paint, in the art room—where art slowly and surely becomes separate from the rest of life. And thus this thing that children naturally do, which is to make universes out of any old thing, is lost because we need them to grow up and do other things, like make one new piece of the front end of a car over and over, and in this way the place where we can "be creative" is reduced and measured by the question: are we good at art? And as we repeatedly ask this question, the living, breathing nature of this insanely powerful childhood creativity is slowly and gradually changed until it has been turned into a very special specimen in a very special box for very special people.

The idea that the children are not in a bubble, that they are completely in our world, that they see, hear, feel and experience all the crap we do, and still they act like this—they marry a milk box and pretzel stick—and they do this while we are freaking out about the world ending, or whatever it is we are freaking out about, not because they are insane but because they are powerful; this is not our story. Our story is that they are in the bubble that is perfect and beautiful and protected by us and we are so nice to do that and we are such good protectors. And child rapists do not come in there, and if they do come in there, they ruin everything forever and ever.

And here we can see that our story is hardly even a story at all, it's more like a tantrum. If child rapists only ruin things for a little while, if we hear on TV, for instance, the miraculous and really almost impossible story that a fifteen-year-old young lady, let's say, has really and truly gotten over being raped, and moved on, then we may say good for her, how amazing, but also deep down perhaps we are a little afraid that by actually getting over her trauma "so quickly," we will lose our story about how evil and bad forever and ever child rapists are. We keep our story at the expense of the rapeee, of course, but we don't really care about the rapeee; we care about ourselves and our story.

It is this story about what childhood is that makes what happened to me—not being raped by a family-sanctioned babysitter, which is totally, banally believable—but my breaking through the fourth wall at a community theater production of "Sleeping Beauty" and, if I may add, doing so not in some spazzy, "Soy Bomb"-MTV-Awards way but in a controlled and planned and joyful way, where I ran onto the stage not because I was ignorant and impulsive but because I was smart and expansive and strong and knew I could save the fucking day, this is not believable.

This is not believable, I understand, because of this agreed-upon reality we have of children in their special childhood time/place, which is not of our world. And because the adult world of "real" problems and the childhood world of insanity/Jupiter dish-scrubbers supposedly never intersect—this is where the child rapist so shockingly transgresses—children are not allowed to be incredibly smart and strong and resilient and powerful in response to our adult world because we really don't believe they ever come in contact with it, which is, when you think about it, a pretty shocking denial.

We cannot see that staging a puppet show with two baby carrots is a sane and powerful response to adults freaking out about the world ending—and if you recall your own childhood you will remember that you always knew when the adults were freaking out, and you also knew you weren't supposed to know—because we cannot recognize that children can be powerful in our world, in response to our world, especially if we know that at the same time they are being powerful, they are also, periodically, being assaulted and/or raped. Because we have already agreed upon what child-rape looks like, and it does not look like children being powerful, thank you very much, it looks like women crying.

And this, I think, would be a good time to talk about what joy is, because now that I am dealing with Ate and addressing things in this book that are not believable, I want to talk about the twin strangers who came to visit me on the ceiling after I was raped, which is a detail I almost did not include in this manuscript because I thought, no one will believe me and I will look like an idiot. But now that I am talking to

Ate and butting up against how little is actually believable, and now that I am seeing just how imprisoned we really are by the idea of what is allowed to happen, I don't care anymore; I am just going to throw everything in and look like a kook or idiot or whatever, because I see now what a miracle it is that anything interesting or spontaneous ever happens in a human life at all.

And I think this would also be a good time to say that I feel joyful about this. I am going to throw it all in, the back and forth and up and down and sideways—all of it. And it is with joy now that I say: thank you, pedophile. Thank you Mr. Dauth, you stupid prick; thank you for making me a writer; thank you for forcing me to be alone with my weird thoughts for so long that I didn't think it was unusual or scary to be different; thank you for helping me to fly out of my body, to know that I could do that and live; thank you for scaring the living shit out of me so that I could be brave; thank you for letting me believe I was a superhero and saving my family from death; thank you for helping me learn how to be really fucking powerful; thank you, you motherfucker, I hope you have fun in hell. Which exists.

8

I have decided that this old idea that I have a body I am inside, like a car, until I die, at which point I open the door and step out, is actually not very believable. What is more believable, I think, is that I have a body and that my relationship with my body changes, and I am inside and outside and around and over and behind my body, and these shifts take place depending on day and time and weather and feelings and who knows what else.

I have still been trying to talk with Patricia about what she is doing. I wouldn't say it is going very well. For awhile I brought a tape recorder and taped our conversations during my sessions, but we talk about all kinds of stuff—recipes and the weather and our husbands—not just What It Means To Touch. We are friends. But the tape recorder seemed to spook her and she would tell me afterwards, when she remembered it was there, to please not to write about X or Y, so I stopped bringing it. Now I just write things down that strike me after I see her.

The last time I saw her she told me that she had been through a period, learning to touch the way she does, where she was afraid she would never be able to touch people and feel nothing again.

"How did you get through that?" I asked her.

"I don't know," she said. "It just passed."

8

The first time I sat on a motorcycle and started it, at the motorcycle safety course three weeks ago, I just about fell over when the bike came on because I could not believe there was this humongous throbbing vibrating between my legs. Any lady who has sat on a revving motorcycle and says she cannot imagine herself having an orgasm on it is lying. I found it hard to believe that we are supposed to sit on these things like this is all natural and normal and not basically like we are riding big vibrators and can barely converse for all the throbbing. But I am doing it. I start the bike and sit on it like, Oh yeah. No biggie.

I am getting ready to sit on the bike again this weekend to retake my test. At night before I go to sleep I have been trying to imagine it. I have been trying to feel how it will feel to get on the bike and not screw myself over.

8

Last night I was putting away the dishes for the nine hundred thousandth time, the same slightly wet cup in the same

place on the shelf. It's a plastic glass with the KOOL logo
on it, for KOOL cigarettes. Frank got it at the flea market.
It's a glass, but it's not made of glass, it's plastic, so it's an
everyday glass. I am not afraid of breaking it. I trash it, basically. I don't care that it's vintage or has an interesting logo
on it or that there's no place to get another one now but
Ebay. It's plastic and I couldn't break it unless I tried very
hard. So I use it every day and I don't care that the logo is
going to eventually rub off in the dishwasher from the heat
and the force of the water. I put it in the dishwasher.

But I also love it, I will be sad when I can no longer put
water and ice in it.

So I was putting the KOOL glass that I love in the dishwasher that is going to destroy it, and as I was putting it
there I was thinking that the biggest lie in the world is the
one where we think because one thing happened it will
always happen. This lie is where Satan lives. I am four years
old now, I believe in Hell, I believe in Satan. I am four and
forty at once right now, and I can tell you: we are unbeliev-
ably powerful. We are shapeshifters. And we know this
because at one time we were small and things happened, and
we went on because we had no choice, and we went on
because we were truly blessed, and more things happened
and we went on, and eventually we didn't walk the same or
talk the same or look the same or sound the same. And then,

meaning now, we are big, and we can do, as the kids say, whatever we want. We can do things we can't imagine.

So many people don't believe this, though. My friend Patrick said after reading this: "It's just the opposite. We can't do things we can imagine—exactly because we know it's imagination. And kids, as far as they're concerned, do do them—because they don't know it's just imagining."

8

I have been writing at the coffee shop next to King's pre-school. I drop him off and then I come and sit here. I like a spot where I can look out the window. Over the past few months, when I look out the window, I have occasionally seen Adam Horovitz, aka Adrock of the Beastie Boys, walking up the street with his hat on sideways.

I love the Beastie Boys; I am a huge fan. But I know the rule: only bother celebrities if you have a good excuse, and I don't have one.

8

Mick was playing the piano last night. By playing I mean he was tinkling the keys softly and tunelessly rather than banging his palms on them. I sat next to him on the bench. He had a serious look on his face. He tinkled the keys for a few seconds, then turned to me.

"This song is called 'Ladies,'" he said.

He tinkled a little longer.

"This song is called 'Different Kinds of Ladies.'"

He tinkled a little longer.

"This song is called 'Different Kinds of Ladies at Night.'"

More tinkling.

"This song is called 'Different Kinds of Ladies at Night in the Morning.'"

More.

"This song is called 'Ladies and Gentlemen,'" he said finally.

8

I don't know which came first—if I was listening more to the Beastie Boys and then realized that I was seeing Adrock walk by on the street outside the coffee shop or if I saw

Adrock walk by in the street outside the coffee shop and then thought hey, I should listen to more Beastie Boys. But in either case, whether I saw Adrock and then listened more or I listened more and then saw Adrock, the movement of these events was the same. They were wavelike in that they seemed to come from nowhere in particular but then gradually gained form and focus, so that as I became more conscious of Adrock walking by, and what he was wearing and how he walked, my listening to the Beastie Boys went from an occasional and absent-minded enjoyment of "The Negotiation Limerick Files," and "Rhyme the Rhyme Well," to an obsessive study of one particular song, which I downloaded from their website, which was an *a cappella* version of "Ch-Check It Out."

The Beastie Boys have these *a cappella* songs you can download from their website for free and the idea behind it is that you can add your own beats to it—you can remake a Beastie's hit with their singing and your own sounds. But when I heard "Ch-Check It Out" I was amazed—I thought this is so much better *a cappella* than the way it was released; this has so much more power on its own, with just words and silence. If you haven't heard the song, the lyrics are fantastic and nonsensical.

Ate tells me we have a two-line limit on reprinting, otherwise I would have all the lyrics here.

Instead, here is a sample from the chorus:

Check-ch-check-check-check-ch-Check it out

Just repeat that over and over in your head until you start
to get a rhythm, and you will have a good start.

Now for the rest of the lyrics I am going to paraphrase; it's
going to make no sense, and it's going to be sort of like a
giant list that goes nowhere but just go with me on this.

Hey, all you people who love Star Trek
My intention is not to stress you out
Hey all you young people who haven't left home yet
Come on out

I'm going to explode your world
I'm going to pinch you
I am making music again
I'm going to lift you up

I've got a pontoon boat
I'm in the Florida everglades
I'm rich
I'm succulent and elegant
I'm like a classic cartoon in reruns

Hey, everyone, Russell Simmons is a jerk
I've got loved ones who keep me from getting too
full of myself

So when I say you and I are equals, believe me
But I can rap way better than you
So I guess we're not so equal after all
I rap so fantastically
you're going to dance your ass off

Check it out!
What's that?
We'll figure it out and we'll have fun doing it
Join us!

I asked the doctor what's wrong with me
He said you have an electrician up your ass
I'm like a scientist, I control my mind
With this method
I am a genius and an excellent rapper

Hey Timbaland and Magoo, you sold out
I am going to play a trick on you
Because I have all powers
I am a magician, mathematician, and engineer
I also like cotton underwear

A la peanut butter sandwiches!
I am flying by you
Don't kid yourself
I am so powerful; you aren't
We are making a record here
We're almost done, chill out

Check it out!

What's that?

We'll figure it out and we'll have fun doing it

Join us!

My name is King Adrock

I hang loose

I am super-creative

You flatter me

I'm classy

Here, MCA, it's your turn

You can't catch me

Don't get upset about it though

I flow

You want to make rap but you can't

Wash and dry your clothes

Polish your car

Tonight we are going out

We're going to look fabulous

You are going to leave home for sure now

You young people

Check it out!

What's that?

We'll figure it out and we'll have fun doing it

Join us!

You can hear that, right? How brilliant it is? It's brilliant, trust me.

There are a lot of little scenes in the song but in general terms it's a song that is saying "Look at this," and then "Join us." This message is essentially the chorus, which is repeated in the song three times, each time sung by a different Beastie Boy, although all three boys join in on the last few words of each line, and then finally, on the entire last line of the chorus, which is the invitation to "join us." ("Let's turn this party out," they say.)

The weird thing about paraphrasing these lyrics—and seeing them on paper—is that the parts of the song I really love—the parts I began to notice when my listening became more focused—are the sounds/words that are not considered the lyrics at all. These little unrecorded—that is, unwritten, not unheard—words/sounds serve a couple of functions. On one hand, they function for the sake of sound only. The very beginning of the song, for example, opens with Adrock growling a long, low-to-high, guttural "Yo—ah!" that basically acts as the ignition for the song. It's the sound of the "Ch-Check It Out" car starting. On the other hand "Yo-ah!" does function as a word—(yo means Hey or hello, but you knew that)—and in that sense does act as a starter, i.e, a greeting or call to attention. But its primary importance here, in terms of meaning, is in its work as a sound, and I think that is true for almost all these little sonic bits that I have become so fond of in this song. In some ways they function more like poetry—a sound that is sense—than the lyrics themselves, which are sometimes browbeaten to an inch of their life by the rhyme (though of course you would not know that from my paraphrase; you can find the real lyrics on the wild west of the internet).

Listening to the song yet again, I have written down these additional sonic-bit lyrics, the ones that are not recorded on any lyric sheet but that impart as much if not more meaning to the song than the proper lyrics themselves, in my book:

Yo-Ah!
Uh-huh
Kumon!
Ah!
Ahhhhhh!
Ah!
Huh?
Ya!
Check!
Ah!
Woo!
C'mon!
Oh!

Ha?
Mmmmah!
Ha!
Mmm!
Ah!
Yay!
Wah!
Uh!
Oh!
Uh! Uh! Now!
Aaaargh!
Mmmm-pop!

The meaning of these words is essentially: I am here. Now you can roll your eyes and say, of course, the meaning of every word ever stated is essentially, at its very root, a communication of the fact that the speaker of the word is present. To utter a sound means: I am here, I am alive.

But in the case of this song, which is an incredibly complex and multilayered presentation of the give-and-take between performer and audience, where the three Beastie Boys take turns as performers for each other, audience members for each other, and performers for us, the necessity for the boys to say, over and over, in twenty-five different ways, "I am here," is important, because who is speaking and who is listening is shifting at such a rate that "I am here" in this song is not just another breast-beating rap-reiteration, (although it is that, too) but a locator, a way of keeping the rapidly shifting identities of the three listener-singers/audience-performers straight. In this case "I am here" means not only "I am over here," but "I hear you." And to say twenty-five different ways, "I hear you," is also giving, in twenty-five different ways, encouragement and support, as any MSW-candidate, therapist-in-training would tell you.

The song really became about this for me. It was the sound of one boy passing off the talking stick to another, saying in sound, "Go on, now, it's your turn, do your best, I'm here, I hear you," and at the same time changing from audience member to performer to audience member, even as all three know all the time that they are all performers in every moment for us. This song, which is really less a song and more an incantation/collage, became, in this way, a very powerful soundtrack, and I was really moved by the message I was hearing in it, of the possibility of change, of fluidity, of how people can change and be there for each other, and I thought: I aspire to that. And they make me feel like I can do it, too.

And then, as I said, at the same time that I was studying this song and loving it so much and feeling that it was encouraging me as I was writing in the coffee shop, I started

seeing Adrock walking down the street, and every time I
saw him I was excited because his music meant so much
to me right then, but I kept not going up to him and
telling him because I am a New Yorker and I know the
celebrity rule. But after the ninth or tenth time I couldn't
stand it anymore and I finally said to myself, the next time
I see him I am going to tell him how much this song
means to me.

And finally I saw him again and it was on the day I had my
full kit on—my pink Beastie Boys T-shirt and the pink
leather clogs I had just taken to the Garment District shoe
guy to have embroidered with INTER (left foot) and
GALACTIC (right foot). And I saw him from inside the
coffee shop as he was passing by and I ran out the coffee
shop door and caught up to him and said, "Adrock," and
was aware as I said it that it was so amazing that I was saying his name in this way that meant, "Hey, slow down." In
all the times I had ever said the word "Adrock" in my life
I had never said it like that before, like a command, and it
was like I was in some alternate universe; I had walked
through some door where I was able to use all my words
in a way that was more powerful. So I ran up to him and
showed him my clogs and told him everything I have just
told you but much more incoherently about how I loved
the *a cappella* "Ch-Check It Out" and how my favorite
part of it was this part I could only hear because it was

a cappella, and that was the part of the boys encouraging each other in their wordplay, and he was very modest and said, "Oh, we encourage each other all right," with a wry smile.

And then we talked a little more and finally I went back into the coffee shop and he went I don't know where. And then I saw him a couple weeks later from inside the shop again and waved at him and he made a gesture like he couldn't stop and I let him go and then King graduated from preschool and I changed writing spots and I haven't seen him again and don't expect to, but this being New York you never know.

8

King's ears still weren't draining, so I took him back to his pediatrician, who told me to take him to the Ear Nose and Throat guy, and even though he was a guy I didn't care anymore: I was sick of this issue. So I took King to the ENT, who was fantastic, I loved him, and he told us that the fluid in King's ears was starting to thicken and that King was operating with a significant hearing loss, so the following week Frank and I and King went to the hospital and the ENT took King's adenoids out and inserted some tiny tubes in his ears, and that was the end of that problem.

I kept taking King to Patricia, though, because she helped him tremendously in other ways. He was late to talk and she helped him to become more verbal, to come out of his shell. And I continued to go myself. I also took Mickey to her when, at ten months, he still wouldn't eat solids. Patricia cleared that up in one appointment. How did she do that? I don't know.

I asked Frank to go to her, too, and he went, and he admitted he felt great when he went there and he thought it was great for our kids, but after awhile he said: I don't know, it's so weird.

So I was egging Patricia on—I was saying, you can't blame people if they dismiss you because you don't explain what you are doing. And again I complained that craniosacral therapists sound like idiots when they talk, and that no one was taking on the work of educating people about this therapy, and she admitted it was hard work to take on because it's asking people to upend their whole view about what is possible.

No one wants to spend time and energy preaching to those who think you're insane, she said.

8

Another cab ride:

This guy picked me up right near my apartment. There was just something about him: he seemed really friendly even though he didn't talk. He was listening to public radio in a way that also seemed to include me—like he was not listening to the radio, he was listening to my silence and the radio. I felt this and felt compelled, then, to say something to him, so I asked him what he was listening to, and he mentioned the program's name and then he said, "This guy does some neat interviews. The other day he had a dowser on."

"What's that?" I asked.

And he told me dowsers are like clairvoyants; they can tell you anything, they can tell you about your health, they can give you readings about how powerful your life force is, or, if you have disease, what kind of disease, in what area of the body. They can advise you, he said.

"Huh," I said.

"I'm a dowser, too," he said.

And then, as he was driving the taxi straight down Ninth Avenue he held up what looked like a regular house key, with the diamond-shaped top and the jaggedy tail. The key was attached to a piece of string and the string was swinging from his hand like his hand was a rear view mirror and the key was a baby shoe.

He held the key a few inches above the steering wheel and watched it swing on its string for a couple of seconds. "My life force is a 98," he said.

"Wow," I said. "That's based on 100, right?"

"Right," he said.

He was still holding the key up, so I asked him.

"Can you read me?"

"Sure," he said, and he smiled and shifted forward in his seat.

He held the key up even higher, and closer to his face, so that it was practically between his eyes, swinging.

"You can do that while you're driving?" I asked.

"Sure," he said.

I sat there as he drove through the green light at the intersection of 24th and 7th Avenue, watching the key swing.

"Your life force is 49," he said.

"49!" I exclaimed.

"Your heart is 62. You have a tendency toward diabetes. Do you eat sugar?"

"Oh, yeah," I said.

"You should stop," he said, "and eat more fresh fruits and vegetables."

"Why is my life force so low?" I asked.

We were almost at my stop. I had taken a cab to a place I could have walked to in fifteen minutes.

"I don't know," he said.

"Should I have another baby?" I asked, meaning a third one. I figured I might as well just ask him everything, since I was getting out.

He looked at the swinging key. "It won't kill you," he said. "But it's not advisable at this time."

I smirked. I thought "not advisable at this time" sounded like the Magic 8 ball.

8

My mom and I have spoken more about her pedophile. I now know where it happened and with who—though again, there is no name for the guy. His name is what his job was: farmhand. He is not a full man with a full man-body, he is smallified.

8

So I passed my fricking motorcycle test, I got an almost perfect score. I kicked motorcycle ass. It was easy this time.

"Why didn't you do that the first time?" Gary, the head instructor, asked me.

I laughed.

Frank passed his test, too. We are happy.

"When can I get a motorcycle?" King asked us.

"When you're forty," Frank said.

8

So Frank and I have our motorcycle licenses now but we still don't have motorcycles. And it's early November and we don't have much time for motorycle/scooter riding before the snow falls.

I don't know whether I want a scooter or not anymore. By the time I took my motorcycle test I liked using the clutch, I liked changing gears; it was fun. I am not sure I want a twist-n-go after all.

But Frank wanted to get something now, right away, something cheap and small we could practice on. So he stayed up late trolling the internet and found us a used starter bike: a 1981 Honda Passport.

The Passport is basically a bicycle—truly, it even has a basket—with a motor. It's no crotch-rocket; it goes maybe 35 miles per hour tops. It also has this thing called a centrifugal clutch, which I am worried about because it's different from the regular clutch lever I learned on and there's no real place to learn how to use a new type of clutch now. Even if I were to practice on it in a parking lot in Queens, I would still have to get it to Queens by driving it through

Manhattan. I don't really want to be figuring out how to use a new kind of clutch while I am also driving in traffic for the first time.

But it's too late: Frank bought it, and it's really cute, it's yellow and he drove it home from the previous owner's place in TriBeCa to our place in the Garment District and brought it up to our apartment in the freight elevator and I sat on it and got Frank to take my picture sitting like that with my arm around King and then I emailed the picture to my friends. And of course the boys can't keep their hands off it and they play with opening and closing the foot pegs and pushing and releasing the brake lever and whatever else they can figure out how to touch—meaning move—even though we say over and over: NO TOUCHING.

8

I am done caring about the whole world now, and whether the whole world knows or cares that there are people who exist who can do unimaginable things with their hands. The whole world will just have to figure it out.

I listen to Patricia talk during King's sessions, and she holds his legs and talks about how this bone or that bone is moving or shifting, and sometimes she closes her eyes as she does this, so I think it seems logical to ask her, "When you touch him, are you seeing things?"

She seems annoyed with me. I think she is tired of talking about this.

"No, I'm feeling things," she says, as if to a tiresome child. "I'm feeling all sorts of things."

I pushed on. "I don't get it," I complained. "I put my hands on King and I feel nothing."

She straightened up. "That's because you have yourself in it," she said.

She turned toward me and showed me her forearms. She held them out palms up, fingers curled in slightly. Then she let her arms drop down mechanically.

"These are levers," she said.

8

So much of living involves all this mechanical crap—things that are built, that break, that need to be fixed. And all of it— all the built-up and broken things and then all tools, and workshops, and hammering, and trying to fix, and failing—all those things, and then how long all that building and breaking and trying-to-fix and not-succeeding-in-fixing takes—oh my God—it's like the world is not a blue globe at all, it's a giant landfill, an ocean of trash sloshing back and forth, and you're a crumpled-up Fresca can crossing that ocean with no arms and no legs and no will and no wit, just a prayer. And of course the moving, breaking, mechanical things are the first things the boys gravitate to, no matter how small or crappy. It's like they know from birth how impossible it all is, how fantastic, how insane, and they forgive it everything, they are just like mothers, they love it, they just love it, they can't be stopped. Girls, on the other hand, generally either ignore it or never stop being annoyed.

So Frank got the Honda Passport and then he bought a motorcycle helmet, and his helmet sort of fits me. And Frank has ridden the Honda Passport out in traffic a few times, and I am feeling how afraid I am of making this transition, from riding in a safe empty parking lot in Queens to riding in Manhattan, and I think if I just go on being afraid like this I'm never going to do it, so finally I decide I just better do it now.

My plan was to get Frank to watch Mick when Mick wakes up at his usual time, which is 6 A.M. My idea was that I would go out on the Passport in the morning, before traffic got bad.

So I had planned this for a Tuesday morning and then the morning came and Mick got up at 6 as usual but then King got up five minutes later when he usually sleeps at least another hour. So I had to leave two boys rather than one and that was much harder, and I didn't get out on my Honda Passport until 8:30 A.M., which is definitely rush hour.

So there I am, out on the corner of 9th Avenue and 36th, and I am sitting on the bike with Frank's helmet on, and there does not seem like much danger of having an orgasm—sitting on the Passport is less like riding a motor-cycle and more like riding a lawnmower. So I am sitting there very somberly on my lawnmower-bike, trying to find a suitable moment to enter the flow of fast-moving, lane-changing, fuck-you-shouting traffic.

And Chandra is there by then, and she is with the boys, so Frank is out on the corner with me, talking, but I don't know what he is saying: I can't see enough or hear enough with his helmet on, it's blocking my senses at a time I need my senses. I have the face shield flipped up to counteract this but it's not helping.

Frank is talking to me and I am sitting on the bike looking

behind me and he is still talking as I twist the accelerator without using my brain about why, and all of a sudden I start going and it's too late now: I've gone, so I have to keep going.

I drive half a block. There is a stoplight. I stop. I am in the middle lane. There are three lanes, maybe four, I'm not sure how many. I am trying to get in the far right lane because I know I am going to take a right turn somewhere, and then go back up 10th Avenue to 36th again.

The light changes and I go, and because I am continuing to try to change lanes, I use my mirrors. This is not only the first time I have ridden in traffic, this is the first time I have ridden with mirrors, because they don't have mirrors on the bikes at the motorcycle safety class because too many people lay their bikes down—as you call an accident—and the mirrors break off. So the bikes at the class have no mirrors and, for the same reason, no turn signals.

Mirrors and turn signals are focal points now. And as I am in my second block of driving, trying to veer between two cabs, thinking—pretty sure, really—that the lady in that SUV is laughing at me because I am wearing a giant, black, cool-dude motorcycle helmet while driving a small yellow motorized bike with a basket on it, my left mirror suddenly starts flapping wildly in its socket, and I try to adjust it but it's impossible, it won't keep still, it's like the screw just suddenly and spontaneously stripped. It's flapping there like some robot hand trying to hail a taxi.

This is going to be a short ride, I decide. I have only gone ten blocks, but I take a right on 25th and then start going back up 10th Avenue. I have to stop for a long time around 29th street, though, because a giant tractor-trailer is attempting to back into a loading dock and it is taking a lot of backing and forwarding to get it positioned correctly, and I am waiting in the right lane next to a Vespa, and I get the thrill of nodding to a fellow two-wheeler—yeah, my mirror is flapping and I have a basket, but I am in the club—and then as the trailer finally finds its slot and gets out of our way I accelerate and find myself literally going neck and neck with a Greyhound bus. It is in the far right lane and I am on its left and trying to pass it so I can take a right turn, and I am accelerating for all I am worth but I can't go fast enough to pass it, and I am scared I am not going to be able to make my turn because not only can't I get into the right lane because of the bus but I can't slow down because another SUV is crawling up my ass, and as I am trying to figure out how big my nonexistent space cushion is my cell phone starts singing its metalicized Hallelujah and I know it's Frank wondering what is taking me so long and did I wreck?

And then, thank God, the bus turns right on 34th, so I can make my turn on 36th and the pedestrians on the sidewalk at my corner look very alarmed as I head right toward them, but then I stop the bike and get off before I jump the sidewalk, and it is then, when I am no longer actually seated on the Honda Passport, when I am pushing it along the sidewalk toward our door, that I accidentally roll on the throttle, and because I have failed to put the Passport in neutral because what I thought was neutral was first, the bike lurches forward and Frank walks out the door of our building just in time to see our Honda Passport driving on its very own into the side of our corner deli, where it lays down, and the disobedient mirror snaps off, and the other mirror shatters, and the white wire basket twists to one side like a grin.

And Frank stands there open-mouthed as I come over and explain that really the ride was OK, this just happened now, and as I am talking Frank helps me lift the bike up and by the time it is up he understands what happened and he looks at me and smiles and I smile back and he says "Good job!" and gives me five.

8

I have been thinking about the word joy, about the fact that it is impossible to separate joy from movement, and that this is why joy is so often associated with dance. Joy is also a word that is completely associated with the Christmas holiday, in particular, with the angels coming down to announce the miracle of Christ's birth—the tidings. Because of the incredible importance of their news, the angels transgressed, they broke the boundaries between heaven and earth, between the seen and the unseen, between the human and divine. But this joy, it seems to me, is less the joy of us humans and more the joy of the angels. They were joyous in telling us there is hope for us after all. After all, we can come and join them. Were we joyous, I wonder? We humans who lived in Bethlehem then? Or did we just think: "oh that's nice, now I have to go feed the donkey"?

I must confess here that my expertise on Christmas and even on the Christian religion is pretty limited; I have celebrated the Christian holidays all my life but with no attention to the religious story behind them. My family never went to church. Easter was about bunnies and chocolate; Christmas was about presents and Santa. I have never attended a church regularly, save for the year-and-a-half that I went to boarding school, which happened to be Catholic, and where I was required to attend Sunday mass, which I did without taking communion, sitting that part out with the handful of Jewish girls attending the school, more in a show of defiance to the nuns, whom I hated, than anything theoretical.

Despite this, and despite some dark adolescent moments, I have pretty much always believed in God, and for this I partly thank my dad who, for reasons unknown to me, insisted on saying my prayers with me each night before bed, from the time I was four or five until the time I was about twelve and told him I didn't want to do it anymore, I was too old for that.

We were not a religious family, as I said, so we had no Bible in our house, and I was hard-pressed, when my dad first informed me that we were going to say our prayers at night, to find a prayer to say. I have Mr. Dauth's Jesus-freak wife to thank for this, then, that the prayer I said with my dad for all those years was one that came from a prayer book for children that she had given me one year for Christmas. The prayer was called "Loving Jesus," and I chose it simply because it was the shortest prayer in the book. My father made no comment on my choice of prayer, or on Jesus, during all the years he knelt beside my bed and heard me recite it. I have no idea whether he believed in Jesus or not. We never prayed at any other time in my family, we never said grace before meals, not even on Thanksgiving. I never heard anyone mention praying as an activity that happened anywhere outside this ritual at my bed every night.

Perhaps because my dad never made any editorial comments on the text I felt free after awhile to start a new prayer after the Jesus prayer. I would complete the Jesus prayer, which was written by someone else, and had lambs in it, and rhymed, and then I would say "Amen" and start a new prayer, which did not rhyme and that was in my own words and that was, basically, a list. It started "And God bless"—God seeming more friendly and accessible than the mysterious and lambified Jesus—and then I simply said the names of everyone I knew, all my friends and family, and all the pets we had, including ones who had died. And then in case I missed anyone, I said "and everyone else in the whole wide world," and then I said "Amen" again.

I was trying to tell you about joy but then I got bogged down in ritual.

I do know a little about joy. Most of it is physical. I know about dancing and figure skating, and having sex, and giving birth. I would say those have been among my most joyful moments. Joy is located in the body.

But this is the trick: joy is outside also.

Joy is a vibration; it includes emotion and body and spirit, all of it.

I felt joy when I skated. What I loved to do most was put

the music on and skate freestyle. It was like dancing with a motor, going faster, turning faster—dancing fast and powerfully and not thinking, listening to music with your body and opening your body to music so the music could be in your body, and not thinking in words.

Falling down sometimes and not caring, jumping and falling and not caring.

The bliss of it being your openness to the thing that was better than you, which was music, which was better and smarter than anything or anyone, ever. The music that explained everything, and letting it in your body and letting your body explain everything. Not thinking in words.

It is a testament to joy's real and frightening power that we have chosen to celebrate a moment of supreme joy and transgression—Christ's birth, the angels' announcement—with a holiday that we have calcified with repetition to such a degree that its traditions are so frozen as to be dead. The real subject of Christmas is not joy at all: it is repetition. Ask anyone who has tried to change a Christmas tradition, who wants to open gifts at a different time, who wants to eat a different meal, put up the stockings in a different place. The "joy" of Christmas is that everything is the same every year no matter what, with the caveat that maybe the toys get bigger and better. Of course many people experience Christmas as a horrible holiday and a therapist I once had told me that this is partly because we expect so much "joy" from Christmas that we get so depressed about what a mess it can be.

Real joy is not anything like Christmas. To be joyful means to take on the properties of the angels—the coming.

Sex is joyful, it is not thinking, it is giving, it is receiving. Cries of ecstatic sex are cries of joy, of disbelief, of shock at pleasure, of travel, of going, of moving, of arrival.

To call the twins who came to me "angels" is to put them in a Christian framework and I don't really want to put them in any framework at all, although it is fine if somebody else does that. Seeing them was not really a joyful experience. It was incredibly comforting, but not joyful.

Were the people who were sinning and poor and sad all those years ago really feeling joy at hearing they had a savior? It gave them some solace, I imagine. It gave them something comforting to think about, it offered some future relief, but I would not call those feelings really joyful.

Maybe it was joyful for the twins in the moment, I don't know.

I am joyful now, though, in telling you that I saw twins, which you could call angels. It happened a long time ago, it's true, but in this joyfuless it is still happening; they came and so they are always coming.

I am taking what I want from the episode I lived through and making a story, and I love the story, I am clinging to it, and the story is that there is a spiritual world and it is of this world and not separate from it.

8

My mom did not visit us for Christmas this year because she doesn't like to travel in winter. She was very generous, though, and sent a lot of money to everyone and a package of things for the boys, including a toy that she surrounded with red and green chocolate kisses and a package of granola bars and two tree decorations that were flat and made of gold-colored metal, a tree and a bell.

At first when I glanced at the toy I assumed it was a kid tape recorder, but looking at it closer, later I saw that it wasn't a recorder at all, there was no place to insert a cassette. It had that shape, though, the boombox shape. And there was a big oval button on it that said PLAY and then three other buttons underneath the PLAY button that were smaller and shaped like a circle, square, and triangle.

These buttons had symbols on them, not words. The symbols were a piece of cake, a shooting star, and something I couldn't decipher—a circle with a half circle on top of it, maybe a space ship.

Each button played a little computerized song. The PLAY button played "Row, Row, Row Your Boat," which is a song I'm fond of, computerized or not. I expected the cake button to play "Happy Birthday" but instead it played something I didn't recognize. The space ship song was also a mystery. The shooting star was "Here Comes the Bride."

I could see why this toy would appeal to my mother. She loves music, and has always loved dancing. As she has gotten older she has started to get that I'm-going-do-what-I-want attitude that old people get, and she told me recently that she went to a shopping mall where a band was playing and she started dancing, she said, because she just felt like it. People clapped and hooted, she said, but she didn't care.

Knowing this about her, I could understand that the fact that this toy played unappealingly uptempo, computerized versions of perfectly nice songs far too loudly, with no volume control, and that the "songs" themselves were so short—"Here Comes the Bride" clocked in at five seconds, "Row Row Row Your Boat' at seven—that they could hardly be called songs at all, was not the point. The point was that my mother wanted to encourage PLAYing, wanted to encourage dancing, and—even though one cannot really dance to a seven-second song, all one could really do, in fact, with this toy was continue to press the buttons like an automaton—I understood that my mother did not want her grandsons to be button-pushing automaton children. She wanted them to dance and sing. So in the end, because it was too loud and grating, I hid the toy from my boys and, instead, I think of my mother when I play "The Numbers Rhumba" for them on our CD player and dance wildly in the living room, and they don't join in at all but look up at me from their trains and trucks with their mouths open, like they can't believe how crazy I am, but they kind of like it, anyway.

8

A healthy relationship with time is something that needs to be taught in school. Time management is not the way, though—that's about looking at time in little increments like money and how you can do X and Y and Z in this amount of time and all the things you can buy with a dollar but that is already a class for believing you are poor and that's not what I am talking about. Children know this, that we are all born rich with time, and we just mess up our relationship with it as we get older, like a boyfriend we mistreat. We hate time and we treat it poorly, we run after it and then ignore it, and it goes on and on. We never love it. We never see it for what it is, because there are always time-management classes and little increments and clocks in the way.

When we are small we do not know time. What we know are actions. What time is it? Time for a story, time for a snack. Time is for spending on actions, and we give ourselves fully to our actions. When we are four it takes a long time to go to the bathroom because there are many things in the bathroom that must be examined. We must examine the toilet paper holder and then the sink and the faucet and the drain plug and perhaps we will plug the drain and then let the water run in the sink until the sink is overflowing and then use the toothbrush to stir the beautiful water and make that beautiful sound of water cascading on the tile floor, and then when the sink is overflowing and the water-cascading sound is constant we will pretend the toothbrush is a diving bird, flying high and then diving down into the water for a fish and then flying high again and then diving down again, and this is not cute or annoying: it is practice for when we get older. Because when we get older time will seem to have stopped because we have children and now we are busy surrounding them, swooping and holding them, enveloping them, ebbing and flowing around them, and in this ebbing and flowing we no longer believe we are going forward, we think no, it is the children who are going forward now, in their relatively straight lines, thank God, as we watch them grow, watch them talk and walk and if they don't walk and talk exactly on time, we get upset, and this is why, in midlife, if we are unfamiliar with this feeling of time-stopping, if it makes us nervous to hover beside the sink for a long time and not think about the clock, we may want to get that feeling of going forward again, and that may be why we may suddenly want to buy sports cars or, um, motorcycles.

8

Vincent De Rosa emailed me because he was back in town. I arranged to have a session with him. It felt good as usual. After it was over I sat chatting with him and I said, "Vincent, for all the times I've seen you, I've never noticed before that you're missing a finger."

"That's because it just happened," he said. It was a couple of months ago, he explained, when he was using a table saw.

I looked at it. It was the pointer finger of his left hand. It was severed between the middle knuckle and his palm. The stump was swollen, and I could see the bone in the center of it, like a little man sitting in a big life preserver.

"I'm sorry that happened to you," I said.

We talked about prosthetics but Vincent said there really isn't one for a finger.

8

Winter is here, it's too cold to ride the Passport now—or it's too cold for me. Frank is riding it to work when it's not snowy. We are planning on going to the big motorcycle show at the Javits Center in January and gawking at all the toys there, dreaming about what we want. Frank wants to get a Kawasaki KLR, he thinks. I think I want to get a Vespa but I also like the Honda Ruckus. But then maybe I want a real motorcycle, too.

In the meantime it's time to wrap Christmas presents. Christmas is in two days, and then my birthday. I am mostly wrapping things for the boys, of course, toy vehicles, mostly: cars, trains, fire and monster trucks.

When Christmas morning comes they actually sleep in. When King gets up I ask him. "Do you think Santa Claus was here?" We look.

He was here. We know from past years, this is what always happens: there are presents, and the carrot is gone.

Thank you

to my mother Dorothy and my husband Frank

to Chandra Sarabjit

to Patricia Codrington

to Vincent De Rosa and Sanghi Choi

to Grave Digger

to Adam Horovitz and the Beastie Boys

to Todd Robbins and Monday Night Magic

to Oksana Baiul

to Paul Hintersteiner and the cabdrivers

to Gary and Antonio of the Motorcycle Safety Foundation
Basic Rider Skills Course

to Dr. Suzanne Rosenfeld and Dr. Robert Ward

to the many friends who encouraged me in this writing. I am particularly indebted to three friends who are also excellent writers: Kathy Giuffre was a very important sounding board for this book and helped me through several key decisions; my longtime friend Patrick Roetzel read and questioned this manuscript with his usual amazing attention to detail; and Andrew Matson encouraged me at a difficult point in the process. I am also very grateful to: Yelena Gluzman, Sharon Anderson, Gilmore Tamny, Bill Burke, Jon Poritz, Lisa Kazaras, and Melinda Moore.

to V Bar; to Joe, James, Fletcher, Enrico, and all the regulars there for the quiet camaraderie.

to The Writer's Room; to Anita Naughton and Patricia Bernard for helping me get a place there.

to the moms of room 401 and beyond: Helen Chang, Eliza Coleman, Kathy Curtis-Hardy, Mari Lazar, King-yee Man, Carol Marquardt, Melissa Robbins, and Annabel Wheeler.

to my excellent agent PJ Mark

to all the fine people at Perseus, especially: John Sherer, Jason Brantley, Nicole Caputo, Chris Greenberg, Brooke Kush,

Josephine Mariea, Julie McCarroll, Jeff Williams, Maris Kreizman, Elena Guzman, Bill Smith, Brandon Proia, Michele Jacob, Laura Shepherd, and Wesley Weissberg.

to Amy Scheibe for her belief in this book.

CB 5/08.

mC 1/08.

6/02

mC